OUTDOOR KITCHEN
IDEAS THAT WORK

OUTDOOR KITCHEN IDEAS THAT WORK

Creative design solutions for your home

LEE ANNE WHITE

The Taunton Press

The Taunton Press
Inspiration for hands-on living®

The Taunton Press, Inc.,
63 South Main Street, PO Box 5506,
Newtown, CT 06470-5506
e-mail: tp@taunton.com

Interior design: Carol Petro
Layout: Viewtistic Creative Partners
Illustrator: Christine Erikson
Copyeditor: Candace B. Levy
Front cover photos: (top row, left to right) ©Scot Zimmerman, Brian Pontolilo ©The Taunton Press, Courtesy Williams-Sonoma;
(bottom row, top left) ©Mark Lohman, (bottom row, bottom left) ©Scot Zimmerman, (bottom row, left to right) Brian Pontolilo
©The Taunton Press, ©Rick Keating.
Back cover photos: all photos ©Lee Anne White, except bottom left photo ©Mark Lohman.

Library of Congress Cataloging-in-Publication Data
White, Lee Anne.
  Outdoor kitchen : ideas that work / Lee Anne White.
      p. cm.
  Includes index.
  ISBN 978-1-56158-958-6
  1. Barbecues (Fireplaces)–Design and construction–Amateurs' manuals. 2. Outdoor kitchens–Design and construction--Amateurs' manuals.
I. Title.

TH4961.5.W45 2007
643'.3–dc22

                            2007020319

Printed in China
10 9 8 7 6 5 4 3 2 1

The following manufacturers/names appearing in *Outdoor Kitchen Ideas That Work* are trademarks: Amish Country Gazebos®, Authenteak™,
Bahama Blue™, Barbecues Galore℠, Big Green Egg®, Big Green Egg®, Bose®, Brinkmann®, BroilKing®, Broilmaster®, Cal Flame®,
Calise™ Outdoor Kitchen Concepts, Inc., Cambria®, Char-Broil®, Charmglow®, Cookshack®, CorrectDeck®, Country Casual®,
Crutchfield℠, DCS™, Ducane® Gas Grills, Dupont®, EarthStone® Wood-Fire Ovens, EverGrain® Composite Decking, Evo®, Fire Magic®,
Fogazzo®, Franklin Chef®, Frontgate®, Fuego®, Gazebo Creations™, Green Mountain Soapstone®, Grill Floss™, Grills to Go®, Hearth, Patio
& Barbecue Association℠, Kamado® (cooker), Kichler® Lighting, Lighthouse Landscape Lighting℠, Lock Dry®, Lynx Professional Grills®,
Maine Cottage®, MECO®, Old World Gazebos®, Outdoor Kitchen® Collection, Outdoor Lighting Perspectives℠, Outdoor Movies℠, Patio
Embers®, Pavestone®, Plow & Hearth®, Primo Grills and Smokers®, Restoration Hardware℠, Safari™, Sea Gull Lighting®, Seaside Casual℠,
Silestone®, Smith & Hawken℠, Solaire® Infrared Grilling Systems, Spirit Elements℠, Summerwood™ Products, The Holland Grill®, The
Phoenix Grill Co.®, TimberTech®, Traeger®, Trex®, Tropitone®, Twin Eagles®, U-Line Corporation®, Unilock®, Vermont Castings®, Viking®,
Weber®, Westminster Teak®

ACKNOWLEDGMENTS

For me, the best part about writing a book is the time I get to spend with so many talented designers. I have always been passionate about design and am fascinated by the creative process. It gives me great pleasure to be able to share my experiences on the road in American backyards with you, so that you might glean some spark of inspiration that can be applied in your own backyard.

I am extremely grateful to the many designers who, over the years, have been so generous with their time, enthusiasm, and knowledge. Each has contributed to my mental idea file and overall understanding of the design process. I could not have completed this book without the tremendous support of Michelle Derviss of Derviss + Chavez Design + Build, Hillary Curtis of David Thorne Landscape Architects, David and Michelle Gordon of Desert Sage Builders, David Gatti and Kym Gatti of P.O.P.S. Landscaping, Ken Whitlow of WaterColors, Gary Passaglia of Simply Outdoorz, Peter deJong of Fired Up Kitchens, Andrew Brodtman of Twombly Nursery, Michael Thilgen of Four Dimensions, James Bairey of Forno Bravo, The Mad Hatter, Barbecues Galore, interior designer Jennifer Romberg, landscape architect Jeni Webber, Jane Taylor of Cottage Garden Antiques, Bill Feinstein of Allied Kitchen and Bath, Chris Romberg of Food Service Equipment, Dan Casanova of Enchantment Custom Builders, and Juan Arzola of J.C. Enterprise Services.

Thank you to the many homeowners who opened their doors to me and to other photographers for sharing your outdoor kitchens with us and with our readers. It was a pleasure getting to know so many of you—frequently over fabulous dinners cooked in your outdoor kitchen.

For their various roles in helping this book come together, whether it was testing products, preparing food, or making introductions, I thank Don Eberly of Eberly Public Relations, Trudy Cooper, my Mom, and my husband—the true master of the grill around our house. And finally, a special word of appreciation to Carolyn Mandarano, my editor at Taunton Books, whose professional manner, thoughtful editing, and encouragement have made this project and others a pleasure.

CONTENTS

Do we really need another kitchen? Admittedly, more than one person posed that question when they heard I was writing a book on outdoor kitchens. But these folks obviously haven't had the pleasure of preparing and cooking food in a thoughtfully designed outdoor kitchen or relaxing and entertaining in a cozy outdoor room.

In truth, we probably don't *need* outdoor kitchens. But I have met homeowners who would gladly give up their indoor kitchens before parting with the one on their porch, patio, or pool deck. These homeowners are spending more time at home with their families and friends than ever before because they've discovered the joy of cooking and entertaining outdoors. And for me, that's the bottom line. An outdoor kitchen is about more than cooking food. It's about spending time with those we love, having fun preparing the food we eat, and rediscovering the natural world that's as close as our own backyards. Besides, you've heard it before—food just tastes better when it's cooked outdoors.

An outdoor kitchen doesn't have to be elaborate. It doesn't have to cost a lot of money. And it probably shouldn't look just like your neighbor's outdoor kitchen. That's because it should be designed based on the way you entertain as much as the way you cook. It may be as simple as a cozy grilling and dining area on a small deck or as complex as a custom-built kitchen with cabinetry and appliances in a poolside pavilion. As long as you use it and

enjoy it and it meets your needs, that's all that matters.

Traditionally, the grilling season lasted from Memorial Day through Labor Day. But thanks to the interest in outdoor living and an onslaught of new products from manufacturers, it's not unusual for folks to grill out year-round now. What we're cooking outdoors has changed, too. It's no longer just burger and hot dog fare. These days, you'll find friends and family roasting chickens, deep-frying turkeys, smoking ribs, simmering a pot of stew, stir-frying vegetables, baking pizzas, and flipping flapjacks outdoors. And rather than retreating to the house when the food is ready, homeowners are spending their evenings under the stars, beneath a fragrant, rose-draped pergola, or gathered around an outdoor hearth.

In this book, you'll find ideas to help jump-start the planning process for your own outdoor kitchen. But even more important, we hope you'll gain a better understanding of the design process, because every outdoor kitchen really is different. We also hope the book will help you become a better shopper, and that if you team up with a designer or contractor, a better understanding of the design process will lead to a more collaborative relationship. In the end, we hope you'll keep in mind that it's really all about relaxing and having a good time with those you care about most.

PLANNING AN

An outdoor kitchen can change the way you think about cooking and entertaining. Creating a comfortable,

OUTDOOR

functional space is more important than which grill you buy, what your table settings look like, or even what you cook.

KITCHEN

Design for the Way You Live

Cooking outdoors means different things to different people. For some, it's tossing burgers on the grill while the rest of the meal is prepared and served indoors. For others, it involves preparing, cooking, and dining al fresco. Some cook outdoors almost daily, whereas others consider it a special activity reserved for weekends and holidays. Before you design an outdoor kitchen, decide what cooking outdoors means, or could mean, to you.

For starters, do you plan just to grill outdoors or might you also consider roasting a whole chicken, sautéing vegetables, smoking a rack of ribs, baking a pizza, or even frying your morning eggs? Would you like to eat outdoors as well, or do you prefer the air-conditioned comfort of your dining room? What will you do after dinner—gather around an outdoor hearth, unwind beneath the stars, or head inside to the family entertainment room?

Next, imagine yourself in your outdoor kitchen. Are you washing vegetables, chopping onions, stirring a pot of soup, or grilling fish? Are you preparing a romantic dinner for two, feeding a family of four or hosting a dinner party for dozens? Which would work best for serving your beverages: a portable cooler, under-counter refrigerator, built-in beverage center, beer tap, or bar with an ice maker? Your responses to these and other questions can help you determine your grill size, counter space, accessories, and seating options.

Dream a little, then make notes, both about what you'd like to prepare in your outdoor kitchen and the kind of equipment and amenities you'll need to pull that off. Think about how much space you might need, what kind of layout would best suit your needs, and how you like to entertain. Most important, think about the kind of space you would enjoy spending time in. Once you do this, you're well on your way to designing a personal outdoor kitchen based on the way you live.

right • When there are activities going on both in the kitchen and out around the grill, a pass-through window with bar seating makes it easy for guests to visit with everyone while dinner is being prepared.

above · Preferring the amenities of an indoor kitchen for food preparation, these homeowners needed only a grilling island and place to dine outdoors. By taking advantage of the covered space beneath a deck, they can grill out in any weather.

below · This full-service outdoor kitchen simplifies lakeside entertaining. The enclosure makes it possible to use interior-grade cabinets and appliances (including a microwave), which can be more economical and come in a broader range of styles than those made for the outdoors. Weather-stripped doors keep the space clean and dry.

Creating an Idea File

Planning an outdoor kitchen addition can be just as much fun as redesigning a room inside your home. Start a clip file—perhaps in a shoe box, notebook, or scrapbook—with images of other projects you like. In addition to the photographs in this book, scour home and garden magazines for good ideas, take snapshots on local house tours, download images and articles from the Web, and pick up catalogs that specialize in outdoor-living products. Obtain paint swatches and outdoor-fabric samples that can be used to create an entire outdoor color scheme. Collect ideas for container plantings, furniture, water features, and other decorative accents that could spruce up your outdoor room. And finally, start a separate box with samples of stone, brick, tile, or other building materials you are considering.

Adding On an Outdoor Room

When these homeowners claimed rooms for his and her home offices, their house suddenly felt much smaller than it had before. They considered moving to a larger place in a new neighborhood, and even spent some time house hunting. But, in the end, they felt their current home was in a good location and they hated to leave their neighbors. So rather than move out, they added on to their existing house.

Unlike most house additions which call for adding rooms with four walls and a ceiling, these homeowners opted to add outdoor rooms—a covered outdoor kitchen with bar seating, open-air dining and living rooms, and a destination seating area for starry nights around a raised fire pit. They've found these outdoor living areas so comfortable that they now spend most of their free time outdoors. In fact, they cook and eat most of their meals outdoors, rarely heating up the indoor oven or stove. Even a breakfast of eggs, bacon, and toast on the grill are standard fare for this couple.

Heating up the gas grill is fast and easy. The side burner is used just like an eye on the stove—making it a snap to cook in a skillet, saucepan, or deep pot. Both the sink and under-counter refrigerator have added to the convenience of cooking outdoors as well. And cleaning couldn't be easier: Counters wipe down quickly; and once a week, the owners hose off everything with a portable pressure washer.

When just the two of them are dining, their favorite spot is on the chairs at the extended bar. When entertaining more formally, the couple opts for a seated dinner at the table beneath a candlelight chandelier. And for casual get-togethers with the neighbors, it's not unusual to find everyone gathered around the fire pit swapping stories about work, the kids, or local happenings.

above • This backyard is set for both entertaining and day-to-day outdoor living,
thanks to the roofed outdoor kitchen
and bar, an arbor-covered dining area, a
comfortable open-air seating area, and a
fun gathering spot around the fire pit.

facing page top • The dining table is used
when the homeowners host formal dinner
parties. As the sun dips below the horizon,
a candlelight chandelier helps create a
magical mood beneath the arbor.

facing page bottom • The extended counter
was designed primarily for casual,
everyday meals. But it doubles as a bar
and works well for serving food and
drinks; it can also be used as a food-
preparation station and is a favorite spot
for working outdoors on a laptop.

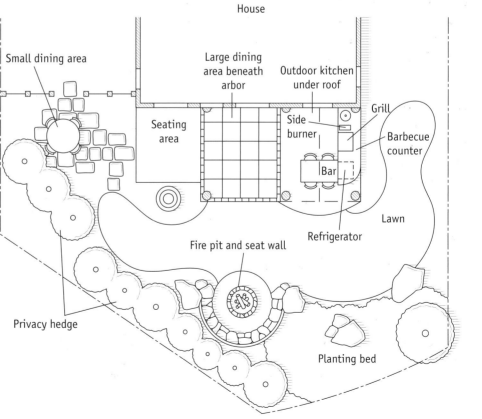

House

Small dining area

Large dining
area beneath
arbor

Outdoor kitchen
under roof

Grill

Side
burner

Barbecue
counter

Seating
area

Bar

Lawn

Refrigerator

Fire pit and seat wall

Privacy hedge

Planting bed

Create a Casual Environment

Cooking and dining outdoors is a casual affair. Outdoors, both hosts and their guests tend to feel more relaxed. Everyone gathers around the cook to socialize, and it's not unusual for guests to pitch in on food preparation or to prepare their own drinks. The environment has a lot to do with it—the fresh air, natural surroundings, and a connection with the outdoors itself.

Outdoor living areas such as patios and decks bridge the gap between a house and the landscape. Even when an outdoor kitchen's design is closely aligned with the home's architecture—common when adjacent or attached to a house—the setting should be comfortable and relaxed, and the materials should be rugged enough to stand up to the abuse Mother Nature dishes out. Rain, pollen, snow, and leaves *will* fall on the countertops. Humidity will cause inappropriate materials to warp or rust, prolonged sun exposure can cause certain finishes to fade, and wind will blow sand and dust into cracks and crevices. For this reason, the best choices in construction materials are those commonly associated with landscaping or boatbuilding rather than interior design.

There should also be a strong connection between the outdoor kitchen and areas devoted to entertaining. Frequently, the outdoor kitchen is the focus of entertaining. Because the chef tends to be the center of attention, give family members and friends a place to hang out and visit by including bar seating, a work island, or small stand-up counter. If you have the counter space, don't be afraid to put others to work shucking corn, chopping salad ingredients, or assembling their own pizzas. This is part of the fun of casual outdoor living.

right • A relaxed dining experience is created by the privacy of the tall plumes of feather reed grass. The Adirondack chairs, with their deep seats, extend an invitation to settle back and unwind, while the wall provides an impromptu seating spot for the chef.

facing page top • Water- and fade-resistant fabrics, all-weather wicker, outdoor carpets and lamps, and durable yet stylish outdoor tables and chairs make it easy to create outdoor rooms that are just as comfortable as those indoors.

right • Rustic, natural materials like wood and stone are ideal for outdoor use. Here they combine to create a stylish cooking pavilion. The stone on the posts and grilling island base cabinets provides a visual link to both the patio and the house.

Backyard Family Fun

With its fabulous views of the California hills, this backyard patio is a great place for a party. But it was designed primarily for day-to-day living and family fun. With three young children, the homeowners wanted a lawn for a play space close by, so they could keep an eye on the kids while cooking dinner on the grill. The table is a great place for games or art projects, and it easily seats six—so there's always room for a friend who may be staying over for the night. The fire pit is a favorite among the kids, who roast marshmallows and make s'mores after dinner or keep warm while telling campfire tales on a cool evening. The parents migrate to the fire pit after the kids have gone to bed and find it's a good way to keep warm even as the fog begins to roll in.

With the deck adjacent to the outdoor kitchen, the homeowners wanted a grilling cabinet that provides ample serving space, storage for grilling tools (especially those used to clean the grill), and a sink. The natural-gas grill is large enough to handle burgers or shish kebabs for a dinner party yet isn't too big for easy weeknight dinners for the family. The sink features a deep basin that makes cleaning large serving platters a snap. It's also just large enough for giving the family dog a bath. The heavy-duty arbor not only adds visual interest and height to the grilling counter but also supports hanging lights that illuminate the grill, sink, and countertop for food prep, cooking, and serving.

right • The steeply sloping lot was graded to place the house, patio, and lawn on a single level, making it easy to keep an eye on children at play as well as to carry food and plates between the indoor and the outdoor kitchens.

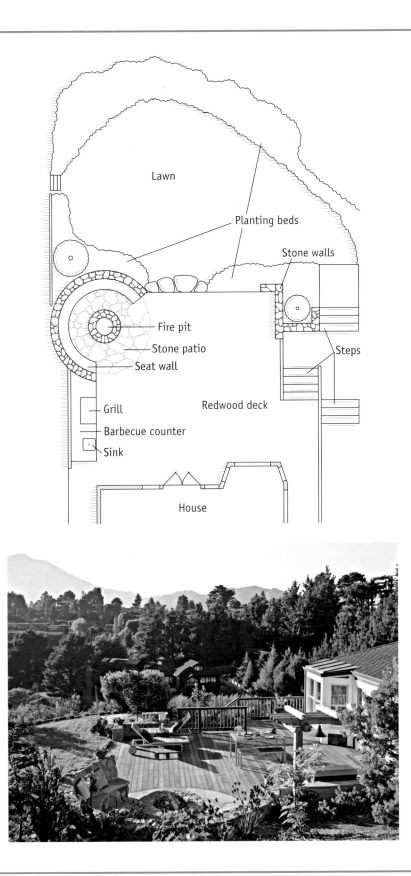

above • The grilling counter and curving seat wall double as a retaining wall for the redwood and flagstone patio. The western red cedar arbor adds an upright accent while providing a support for task lighting.

left • The grilling cabinet is finished in a local flagstone and features a gas grill, stainless-steel sink, and GFCI (ground-fault circuit interrupter) outlets. The drawer beneath the grill is used for storage but is sized so that a warming drawer could be added in the future.

Choose the Right Location

An outdoor kitchen can be built anywhere you like. While just beyond the kitchen door is the most common and often the most practical location for its convenience, it's not the only choice. Poolside is also a popular location—whether on the pool deck, beneath a shady pavilion, or inside a pool house. Some outdoor kitchens are built along the far edge of a deck or patio, where they take advantage of special views or feel more like they are part of the landscape instead of the house. Occasionally, they are placed even farther away as a destination or retreat in the landscape. In the city, a rooftop or balcony may be the only option for outdoor cooking and dining.

While just about anything goes, there are a few practical matters to keep in mind when choosing a location. First of all, the closer you are to the house, the easier and less expensive it will be to tap into utilities such as water, electricity, and natural gas. Also, the closer you are to the kitchen, the fewer amenities you typically need to include in your outdoor kitchen. If it's not easy to dash inside for plates, a cold drink, or to wash the dishes, you may need to include extra storage, a refrigerator, and dishwashing capabilities in your outdoor kitchen.

Also remember that *out of sight* can also mean *out of mind*. If you can't see your outdoor kitchen, you may not use it as often. Build it where you'll feel compelled to pick up the grilling tongs and head outdoors every time you glance out the window.

above • This thatched hut is a popular destination in the landscape. Equipped with a portable bar, it is a favorite place to serve drinks, entertain friends, and escape the heat of the sun. It also helps draw guests out of the house and toward the pool during parties.

facing page • Located halfway between the pool and the house, this outdoor kitchen and hearth offers the best of both worlds. It's close enough to the house for convenience but truly provides an outdoor atmosphere since it's next to the water.

right • Spots adjacent to game areas like this bocce ball court are excellent for cooking and dining. However, if you anticipate a rough-and-tumble activity, like football or volleyball, there should be a generous distance between the cooking/dining and the playing areas for safety.

Evaluating Your Site

Any number of backyard locations are suitable for an outdoor kitchen. The key is figuring out which one works best for you. For quick weeknight dinners or just grilling out, a spot not too far beyond the kitchen door is usually the most convenient. For entertaining outdoors, patios and decks are good choices. If shade or cover from rain is desired, seek out a portico, porch, or pavilion. And if you spend a lot of time around the pool, a pool house or the pool deck may be your most logical choice.

Beyond use, think about what utilities you may need. Is there an easy way to tap into existing power, water, or gas lines or will new lines need to be laid? Trenching in utilities is almost always possible, but it is expensive and may require digging up existing landscaping. Consider the terrain: A flat site is the easiest and least expensive to build on, although sloping sites can be terraced or decked. And don't forget to check on any local variances or setback requirements that might restrict an otherwise desirable location.

Shelter and screening—whether provided by the house, trees, hedges, or fences—are important when dealing with prevailing winds. You don't want the wind to extinguish the fire in your grill or blow smoke into your gathering areas. Depending on local conditions, you may or may not want a breeze to blow through your gathering space. Screening will also offer a greater sense of privacy—whether blocking views into or out of your outdoor kitchen.

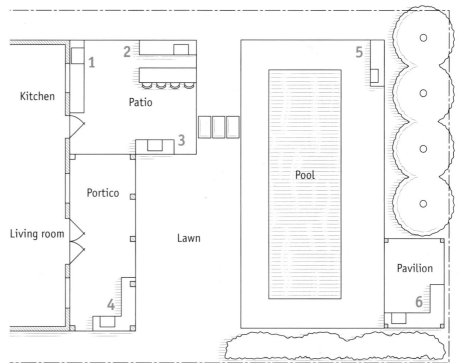

Potential Locations for Outdoor Kitchen

1. Against house
2. Patio corner
3. Edge of patio
4. Beneath portico
5. Pool deck
6. Pool pavilion

facing page • Sometimes the best place is the *only* place—like in this small, urban backyard. In such tight spaces, market umbrellas are a practical choice for creating shade and privacy. Portable grills and furniture can be easily shifted, making the space quite flexible.

right • Although the existing courtyard wall could have served as a backdrop for this outdoor kitchen, the custom tile work behind the grill creates an attractive focal point and provides a better windbreak. The walls create a private area for cooking, dining, and entertaining.

Casual Poolside Entertaining

Although the homeowner had grown up on this property, she found that when she moved back years later with her own family, it was time to update the pool and re-envision the space based on today's lifestyle. What she wanted was a retreat with a comfortable, informal feel—a place she could entertain family and friends any night of the week. As it turns out, the family uses the redesigned space almost *every* night of the week for 10 months of the year. That's because it's not only comfortable but also functional.

While the pool shape remained intact, just about everything else changed. The pool was refinished, and a broad bluestone patio replaced the original concrete deck. The architect designed a poolside cabana that, along with a stone barbecue counter designed by the landscape architect, serves as a true satellite kitchen with a grill, basic appliances, a sink, and plenty of storage space to minimize trips to the house. It even has a wall-mounted television so that the sports-minded members of the family can keep up with games while grilling dinner and spending the day around the pool.

For entertaining, the patio space needed to be flexible. A teak table works for weeknight family dinners and can be expanded for small dinner parties. The pool deck is broad enough for folding tables and chairs, as the couple often hosts dinner parties for 25 or 30 people. There is room on the upper lawn for a band or game of croquet, and the lower lawn is sized just right for bocce ball. When it comes to relaxing, a raised spa closer to the house and a matching raised fire pit anchoring the far end of the pool deck near the seating area provide options. The space is finished off with lush, English-style gardens. The compelling footpaths make it hard to resist a casual stroll among the flowers.

above • When an outdoor kitchen is placed at a distance from the house, storage becomes important. This cabana features shallow, space-saving shelves for barware, blenders, beverages, and paper goods. Drawers under the bar counter hold utensils.

top left • The raised fire pit and low seat wall make it possible to linger outdoors when entertaining—something the homeowners do frequently. The patio was sized to accommodate large parties, yet remain cozy enough for family dinners.

bottom left • The cabana and adjacent barbecue counter create a true satellite kitchen. The cabana is equipped with a sink, refrigerator, ice maker, bar stools, and wall-mounted television. The barbecue counter features a large grill, side burner, and warming oven as well as ample counter space.

facing page bottom • The gently sloping site was graded to create distinct levels that better define the outdoor rooms and create a framed view from the garden to the house. The broad steps provide a graceful transition from the outdoor kitchen and dining area to the garden below.

Consider Your Conditions

Climate is a major factor when it comes to planning an outdoor kitchen. What works in the arid Southwest might fail in the conditions in the humid Southeast. What qualifies as quality construction in Florida might not survive its first winter in northern New England. Designed with an eye to local conditions, an outdoor kitchen can actually extend your season for outdoor enjoyment by weeks or even months.

To get the most from your outdoor kitchen, start by considering your challenges. If you can address those, you're well on your way to creating an inviting space with long-season interest. If flying insects are bothersome, consider a screened area for dining and install fans near the cooking area. Fans also help keep things cooler in hot climates, as do overhead shade structures and misting systems. In hot climates, it may be preferable to build an outdoor kitchen next to the pool rather than just beyond the back door. Where the grilling season is short or evenings cool off early, include an outdoor hearth or patio heater and build screening to divert prevailing winds. If unexpected showers are common, construct a structure overhead so the weather won't derail your plans at the last minute.

The climate and the local availability of materials also affect your choice of construction materials—whether it's for patio flooring, kitchen cabinetry, or countertops. Select rugged materials that can withstand your unique climate conditions—such as intense sun, high humidity, or extended freezes. In terms of universal appeal, stone is the most durable and most commonly used material in outdoor kitchens. It will withstand just about any outdoor conditions, yet even stone's availability varies by region of the country. Local stone will be more affordable than stone from other parts of the country; plus it usually looks the most natural in an outdoor environment. But wood, brick, tile, or concrete may better suit the architecture of a home and, in many cases, is a more economical and environmentally friendly choices—especially where local stone is not readily available.

above • Bluestone may be ubiquitous in New England, but it is extremely durable and offers rugged good looks perfectly suited for any backyard patio. This stacked-bluestone grilling island features a dropped counter, putting the side burner at a comfortable working height.

right • Wind poses a greater threat than rain or snow on this exposed California hillside. The raised backsplash and narrow, yet sturdy arbor help reduce the draft along this courtyard wall where the outdoor kitchen is positioned.

Mosquito Control

Mosquitoes, and the diseases they carry, are a real problem during warm weather in many parts of the country. Because prevention is usually the best measure against mosquitoes, any areas of standing water, from gutters to birdbaths and water features, should be routinely checked and cleaned.

Although repellents used sparingly on skin or clothing help keep mosquitoes from biting, other technologies can provide relief as well. Ultra-low volume (ULV) foggers, which disperse a water-based botanical insecticide, can be used to spray an area for temporary relief from mosquitoes. Devices that lure, trap, and kill mosquitoes can be installed, though some are expensive to operate. In addition, their effectiveness depends on the mosquito species, breeding habitat, population size, wind velocity and direction, an individual's tolerance level, and other factors. Mechanical barriers such as screened or glassed porches are often good choices for locations with high mosquito populations. And a good ceiling or floor fan will do wonders for keeping these pesky insects at bay.

The ceiling fan in this cozy covered patio does more than provide a refreshing breeze on a hot summer day. It helps keep mosquitoes, gnats, and other flying insects at bay by circulating the air.

Weathering the Elements

Few places, if any, have perfect year-round weather. In the South, spring is glorious, but it is followed by hot, humid summers. That doesn't keep local residents from enjoying outdoor activities in summertime, but it does provide an incentive for making outdoor living areas as comfortable as possible. These homeowners figured out how to do just that.

A dip in the swimming pool, which is located just beyond the patio, is a refreshing way to cool off any time of day. And the covered patio, or portico, provides much-needed relief from the sun as well as a place to relax or cook dinner. But it can get hot even in the shade, so a ceiling fan keeps the air circulating in this room, making it feel a good 5 degrees to 10 degrees cooler. There are other fans as well. Two large drum fans (the kind you see on the sidelines at football games) and a pedestal fan keep air moving on the patio, which is especially nice when dinner is being served. The fans also help keep annoying insects away. They are positioned for good air circulation rather than for blowing directly into seating or dining areas.

Fall temperatures fluctuate widely, but it's generally prime time to be outdoors. Again, the portico is the place to be with its stacked-stone hearth and dinner sizzling on the grill. Cooking outdoors is even possible through most of the winter—thanks to the roof to keep out the rain and the ceiling-mounted heaters to help keep the space warm and comfortable.

top right • This portico stays comfortable year-round. High ceilings allow the hot air to rise, while a ceiling fan keeps air circulating on warm days. When temperatures plummet, ceiling-mounted heaters and a fireplace keep the room cozy.

right • Several drum fans are placed on the patio and around the pool deck to keep the air moving on those hot southern days when humidity hangs in the still air. They run on standard household current.

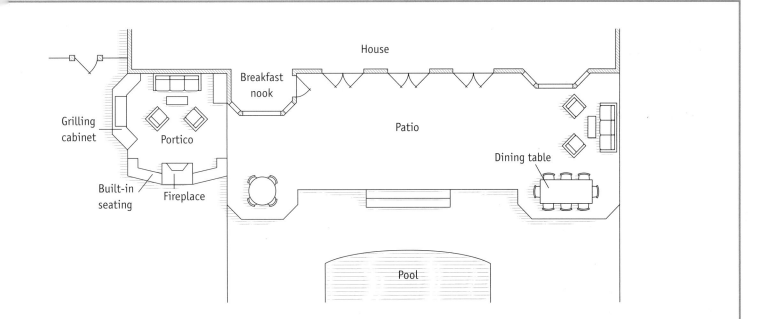

House

Breakfast nook

Grilling cabinet

Portico

Patio

Built-in seating

Fireplace

Dining table

Pool

above • This granite counter sits atop a stacked flagstone base that matches the outdoor hearth. It doubles as a food prep and serving counter and helps block the grill from general traffic—a decision made for both safety and aesthetic reasons.

right • The outdoor fireplace is flanked on both sides by built-in bench seating, which is softened with pillows. Although its primary purpose is to create a wall between the room and the garden, the extra seating is appreciated during large gatherings.

Budget Realistically

Adding an outdoor kitchen is a lot like renovating a room inside your home. If you keep it simple and do much of the work yourself, you can often design on a dime. On the other hand, you can easily spend as much as you would on an indoor kitchen by choosing custom cabinetry, top-of-the-line appliances, and a full range of accessories. If you're installing a patio, deck, or pool house with landscaping at the same time, count on it costing considerably more. Design, labor, construction materials, appliances, and landscaping costs can add up in a hurry, but they don't have to. Most outdoor kitchen projects fall somewhere between these two extremes.

Manufactured grilling islands with stucco or cultured-stone veneers, tile countertops, and modestly priced drop-in grills start as low as $1,000 but can easily escalate to more than $10,000 when custom-built with natural stone facades, polished-stone countertops, and six-burner stainless-steel grills with all the bells and whistles. Custom cabinetry with top-grade materials, commercial-grade appliances, and challenging construction sites all increase costs.

Visit home centers and specialty grilling stores or shop online to get a feel for the cost of materials. Talk with several experienced designers and construction firms for ballpark estimates and suggestions before you get too far into the planning process. Also, prioritize your wish list so that you can make smart decisions as the design process progresses. The more you know before you start, the smoother the process will go and the easier it will be to stay on budget.

top right · For this outdoor enthusiast, there are few experiences more enjoyable than a relaxed evening spent around the campfire and picnic table with good friends. Food is cooked in a cast-iron pot over the fire as well as on a nearby grill.

right · Many barbecue and fireplace shops offer economical framing systems that can be varied in length; adapted for different inserts; and custom-finished in stone, stucco, or tile. This 54-in.-wide grilling island features a cultured-stone veneer and flagstone countertop.

facing page · Big ideas don't necessarily require big budgets. These homeowners started with a basic firebox kit and built their own unique pizza oven, which has become a centerpiece in their backyard landscape.

Choosing a Design/Build Team

Outdoor kitchens are a relatively new phenomenon. For this reason, firms that specialize exclusively in the design and installation of outdoor kitchens are just beginning to open their doors. You'll find many more types of firms design or build outdoor kitchens as a sideline to their principal business. This is why it's important to see samples of their work, to ask lots of questions, and to talk with their clients before signing any contracts. You want to make sure a particular designer or contractor can build the kind of outdoor kitchen you're looking for rather than to have your choices of layout, materials, or appliances be limited by their experience.

Many outdoor kitchens are designed by architects and constructed by homebuilders when building a new home. These firms can form a strong partnership if you're building a house from scratch, but few handle outdoor kitchens as an add-on feature to an existing home. For this situation, residential landscape architects, kitchen designers, and home remodeling contractors offer the most experience. In some cities, specialty retail stores sell and install modular and manufactured outdoor kitchen units. Also, you may find craftsmen who have mastered the art of building wood-burning ovens or outdoor grilling islands. Ask around for recommendations, especially if you have friends with outdoor kitchens.

Another option is to serve as your own general contractor, pulling together a team of designers and independent craftspeople to complete the task—thus making the most of each of their experiences and talents. If you take this approach, make sure you've consulted local building codes and acquired any appropriate building permits, as these often apply to outdoor kitchens. The scope of the project, the local market, and your own level of desire for involvement all play key roles in choosing an appropriate design/build team.

above • By employing the services of a landscape designer, these homeowners ended up with an outdoor kitchen that blends in almost seamlessly with the landscape. Plantings and terracing help screen the grilling island, and the patio follows the gentle curve of the streambed.

facing page • Designed by the homebuilder, this outdoor room exudes the warmth and comfort of an indoor room. The veneered stone wall and fireplace mantel extend into the house, creating a strong visual connection between indoor and outdoor spaces.

DESIGNING

There are very few rules when it comes to

designing an area for cooking outdoors.

A KITCHEN

The outdoor kitchen that works best is simply the

one that satisfies your needs. No more and no less.

THAT WORKS

Visualizing the Space

Once you've settled on your basic needs for cooking, dining, entertaining, and related outdoor activities, it's time to start thinking about the space itself. Where will it be? How big will it be? And what will it look like? It's also important to think about how you want the space to feel. Should it be open to sunshine, gentle breezes, and special views or would you prefer a cozy setting with an outdoor hearth, a roof overhead, and ample screening for windbreaks and privacy?

When planning, it's helpful to think in terms of "rooms." By carving a small backyard into two or three rooms, that same space suddenly feels much larger. And the same strategy works equally well for large properties: Breaking them down into a series of smaller spaces makes them more inviting and more manageable. Doing this is a lot like creating multiple seating areas in a large living room or different living areas in a loft. Also, by thinking in terms of outdoor rooms, you can start to visualize the floors, walls, ceilings, and passageways that are just as important as those inside a house—even if they're only implied by a tree branch overhead, a post on an arbor, a low seat wall, or series of pots on a deck. And although you have considerably more flexibility outdoors than indoors, it's sometimes helpful to measure dining rooms, kitchens, and family rooms to get a rough estimate of how much space you need for similar activities or to accommodate furniture outdoors.

The other factor you want to consider at this point is style: Should your outdoor kitchen and adjacent spaces relate more to the house or the landscape? Or is there an entirely new theme that you'd like to create outdoors? The style selected—whether sleek and contemporary, traditional, or eclectic—will guide you in making decisions on building materials, furniture, and landscaping.

right • By taking advantage of the adjacent indoor kitchen, the size of this grilling cabinet could be kept to a minimum, freeing up remaining covered space for a cozy seating area and fireplace rather than counter space or storage.

above · The grilling cabinet and kiva-style fireplace form the exterior walls of this portico, giving the homeowners plenty of flexibility for arranging furniture. Extensions can be added to the teak dining table to accommodate additional guests without feeling cramped.

left · With a low profile and stone cabinetry, this outdoor kitchen blends right into the landscape. The curved extension offers a convenient spot away from the heat for friends to hang out with the chef while dinner is being cooked.

Ten Guidelines for Outdoor Kitchen Design

1. **Make It Convenient.** Design an outdoor kitchen in a location where you're most likely to use it. An outdoor kitchen just beyond the back door is easily accessible, but don't hesitate to build it by the pool if that's where you spend your time.

2. **Create a Casual Setting.** Outdoor kitchens are all about relaxing and having fun outdoors. Design a kitchen with counters for guests to lean on, bars to pull up to, or a comfortable seating area close by.

3. **Plan Ahead for Utilities.** Utility lines should be run before a patio is paved and cabinets are installed. Keeping runs short for utility lines will save money. Away from the house, propane tanks or charcoal grills might be more economical than natural gas, and a small hot water heater located beneath the sink is the easiest way to provide hot water, if needed.

4. **Select Durable Materials.** Indoor materials may not last a season outdoors. Build cabinetry from materials that won't rust, rot, or warp. Choose countertops that won't crack, delaminate, fade, or scratch badly. Select appliances, lighting, fans, and sound systems specifically rated for outdoor use.

5. **Build Everything to Shed Water.** Design roofs, floors, and countertops so that they slope at least $1/4$ in. every 2 ft. so that water will run off. Paved surfaces may also need drains; and because wind can drive rain even into tight spaces, weather-stripping and installing drains in base cabinets are good ideas in wet climates.

6. **Provide Shelter from the Elements.** Roofs, pergolas, awnings, and umbrellas all give some level of protection from either sun or rain. Walls, fences, trellises, and plantings can provide much needed windbreaks.

7. **Install Ample Lighting.** A mix of functional and accent lighting will make an outdoor kitchen safe and inviting. Task lights will make food preparation, cooking, and eating much easier. Placing lights on separate switches and dimmers will give you the greatest control over ambiance.

8. **Ventilate Smoke.** Few things run off guests faster that unwanted smoke and fumes. Grills should be placed downwind of prevailing breezes and at least 4 ft. from serving, dining, and entertaining areas. Commercial-grade hood vents are essential for covered grills on a porch or portico.

9. **Design for Easy Cleanup.** Select materials that can be cleaned and maintained easily, such as those with smooth, nonporous surfaces. A nearby garden hose will simplify matters considerably, as will a portable power washer.

10. **Make It Easy to Winterize.** Although year-round grilling is possible just about anywhere, homeowners in colder climates will want to shut off water and gas lines when temperatures drop below freezing. Making shut-off valves easily accessible will simplify matters considerably.

facing page • Since the cooking and dining areas share a cozy corner of the patio, the grill was positioned in the far corner to minimize heat and smoke. The sink is positioned more conveniently for food preparation, bar needs, and basic cleanup.

PORTABLE OR PERMANENT

Outdoor kitchens can be created with portable fixtures, permanent fixtures, or some combination of the two. Portable grills, bars and worktables on casters, and light-weight furniture offer flexibility—an ideal solution for hosting different types of gatherings. They can be carried along if you move. And most portable fixtures are less expensive than their built-in counterparts (though they come in a full range of quality grades and price ranges), making them a practical choice for those on a tight budget or phasing in construction over several years.

Permanent fixtures—cabinets with built-in grills, appliances, and perhaps bar seating—are built for the long haul. The cabinets offer protection for the appliances, increase storage capacity, and provide an enclosure for utility hookups. Permanently constructed outdoor kitchens can also increase a home's value.

COVERED OR EXPOSED

Regardless of location, outdoor kitchens can be either covered or open to the sky. In fact, it's a good idea to provide both covered and uncovered spaces for maximizing the benefits of sun and shade.

In many parts of the country, providing some sort of shelter over a grill—whether a back-porch roof, simple shed dormer, portico roof, or pavilion—is essential to keep unexpected showers from ruining a dinner party. While the meal can usually be moved indoors, the grilling must still take place outdoors, and a roof will keep the grill, food, and chef dry. A dining area under the roof of a portico, on a screened porch, beneath an oversize market umbrella, or in a pavilion offers protection against the blazing sun or sudden showers. Ceiling fans will help keep roofed spaces cool, and heaters, lights, and stereo speakers can be mounted on walls, posts, or ceilings to create just the right atmosphere.

above • Recessed into closet space, this brick alcove helps protect the grill from the elements—though the chef will have to bring his own umbrella on a rainy day. It doesn't occupy floor space, so it's a smart space-saver for small patios.

facing page top • The grill is sheltered beneath the broad eaves of the house so that cooking can continue even in a light rain shower. For shade, dense vines such as wisteria can be grown along the pergola beams.

facing page bottom • Portability reigns around this pool deck. A flatbed grill on casters; a lightweight, cloth-covered table; tall candle stands; and even the sink—which is built into the table and hooked to a garden hose—can be easily rearranged to suit the weather or special occasions.

Making the Most of a Small Backyard

When a client's wish list exceeded the space available, this designer had to get innovative. The available space between the house and a 6-ft.-high retaining wall was a mere 15 ft. deep by little more than the width of the house. Yet the owners wanted a swimming pool, spa, outdoor kitchen, dining area, fireplace, water feature, and room for the kids to play. It sounds impossible, but the designer made every inch of space count.

Since the retaining wall couldn't be removed for budget reasons, she designed everything to abut the wall, which greatly approved the overall appearance and freed up the space between the wall and house for moving about the patio on foot, on tricycle, and with baby-doll carriage. A pint-size plunge pool is perfect for cooling off and for the children to play in; and with water spouts on the adjacent wall, it doubles as a water feature. The fireplace is surrounded by built-in bench seating, which also serves as a step up to the raised spa. A single barbecue counter was built along an end wall, where it occupies minimal space yet offers plenty of amenities: a grill, sink, refrigerator, and lots of counter space. There's even a small patch of lawn on the opposite end of the yard, and just enough room for a four-person dining table on the patio. Wood storage was tucked beneath the fireplace hearth.

By dividing the space into three distinct areas—the kitchen/dining room with hearth, the swim and spa area, and the small lawn, the designer made this shallow backyard feel more spacious.

This fireplace was designed based on traditional Rumford standards, which call for a shallow firebox that reflects radiant heat out into the "room" rather than allowing it to flow up the chimney. The stucco finish matches the home's exterior.

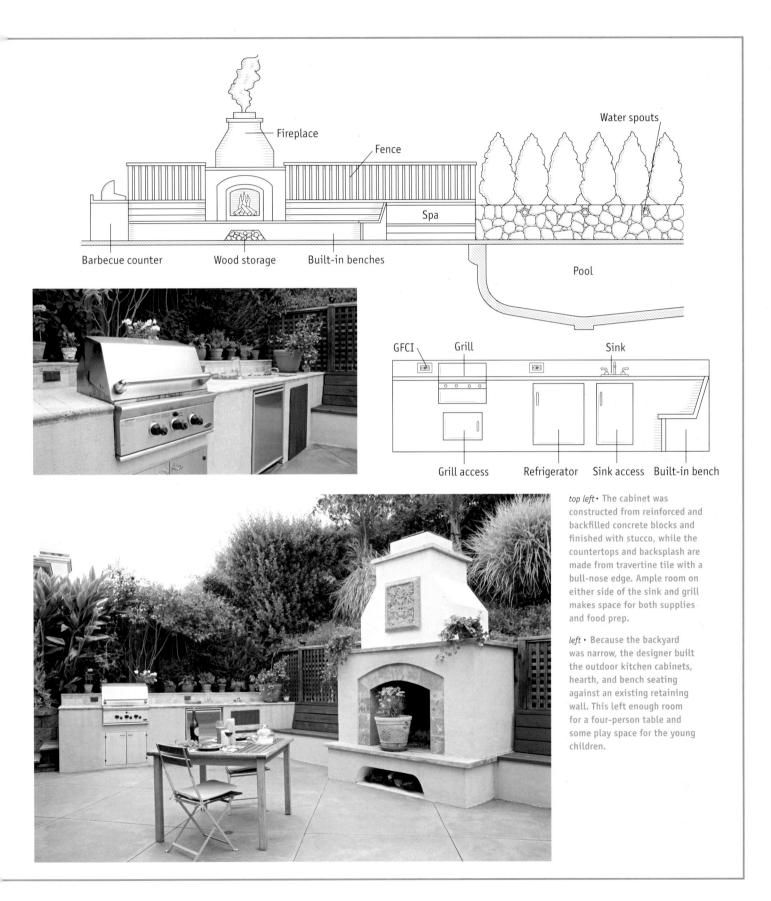

Fireplace

Water spouts

Fence

Spa

Barbecue counter

Wood storage

Built-in benches

Pool

GFCI

Grill

Sink

Grill access

Refrigerator

Sink access

Built-in bench

top left · The cabinet was constructed from reinforced and backfilled concrete blocks and finished with stucco, while the countertops and backsplash are made from travertine tile with a bull-nose edge. Ample room on either side of the sink and grill makes space for both supplies and food prep.

left · Because the backyard was narrow, the designer built the outdoor kitchen cabinets, hearth, and bench seating against an existing retaining wall. This left enough room for a four-person table and some play space for the young children.

ATTACHED OR FREESTANDING

Outdoor kitchens can be attached to a house or built as freestanding elements in the landscape. Both have their advantages and disadvantages. The key is figuring out which best suits your needs and budget.

An attached outdoor kitchen makes it easier to tap utility lines and may make it possible to locate shut-off valves for gas and water inside the house. House walls may provide shade or shelter from wind and light rain and are a good place to mount task lights and speakers. Attached kitchens should be carefully designed to blend into the home's architecture, with matching or complementary materials, consistent rooflines, and similar styling.

Freestanding kitchens may be located on a deck or patio, in a walled courtyard, or around a pool. They may also be designed as a special backyard retreat, perhaps over-looking a special view. Trenching in utility lines for a freestanding kitchen is more expensive than for attached types, but a freestanding kitchen tends to create a stronger outdoor living atmosphere as a compelling destination in the landscape; plus, design options are more flexible when the structure is separated from the house.

Regardless of whether they are attached or freestanding, outdoor kitchens are most convenient when positioned near the indoor kitchen. Food, beverages, and dishes can be stored indoors and brought outside as needed. Dirty dishes can be easily carted back inside and placed in the dishwasher. The farther from the house the outdoor kitchen is located, the better equipped it must generally be. Sinks, refrigerators, and storage space all become critical elements in the design, and wagons or carts are essential for hauling supplies back and forth.

right • This freestanding, stone grilling island helps define the patio and visually connects it to the landscape beyond. The dining table is located closer to the house, which is convenient for bussing dishes.

facing page • This outdoor kitchen features a generous expanse of counter space that is ideal for buffet-style food service. The arrangement works well for catered affairs, because the adjacent indoor kitchen is easily accessed for food preparation, refrigeration, and storage.

above • This dining area is located near the kitchen, which features a convenient pass-through window that simplifies setup, cleanup, and serving meals. A granite ledge was built beneath the window to support goods as they are passed back and forth.

ADJACENT SPACES FOR DINING AND ENTERTAINING

Adjacent spaces designated for dining, relaxing, or entertaining can be just as important as the cooking area itself. In fact, these spaces frequently do more to set the tone for outdoor living than the outdoor kitchen. Chances are, you and your guests will spend more time outdoors if these spaces are comfortably designed and furnished.

When possible, create both sunny and shady seating areas that can be enjoyed in different seasons and at different times of the day. A series of small outdoor rooms will also accommodate different types of activities and different size gatherings. Larger spaces that host a crowd yet offer a cozy corner for an intimate dinner are among the most flexible of spaces. For tight spaces, built-in bar seating is a great space-saving alternative to dining tables and chairs.

While it is perfectly acceptable to remain at the table for after-dinner conversation, a comfortable seating area nearby will encourage guests to linger outdoors longer and can be an inviting destination any time of day. Enhancing the space with container plantings, a water feature, accent lighting, outdoor hearth, or stereo speakers can result in a room that rivals anything indoors for comfort.

Privacy is essential for comfortable outdoor living. If the location, house, or existing landscaping doesn't already provide a place were you can relax without others looking on, then plan for screening—in the form of a fence, wall, hedge, or some type of overhead structure such as a pergola, sailcloth canopy, or roofed pavilion.

above • With multiple dining and seating areas both beneath the pergola and on the sunny patio, it's easy to migrate from one space to another as the temperature rises and falls, or to entertain a crowd.

facing page • A pergola loosely creates walls and a ceiling surrounding the outdoor dining area on this large patio. In summer, the vine-covered pergola and ceiling fan help keep things cool; in other seasons, the hearth helps keep the area warm.

Outdoors from Dawn to Dusk

For these homeowners, the day begins and ends in the backyard. There's plenty to do outside during the in-between hours as well. They often start with breakfast for two at the small stone-topped table where they can enjoy the reflections in the pool. On sunny days, they go for a dip in the pool and bask in the sun on the pool deck. As the day heats up, they can retreat to chaise longues beneath a jumbo-size market umbrella.

Before-dinner drinks and appetizers are served at the grilling counter bar, where everyone can visit as dinner is being prepared. Dinner itself, however, is usually served at the big table beneath the pavilion. Here, ceiling fans help keep the air circulating and a fire is built in the raised fireplace on cooler days to keep things comfortable. After dinner, everyone either migrates to the cushioned seating area beneath the pavilion, takes a relaxing soak in the spa, or sits on a garden bench and gazes at the stars. All in all, it makes for a near-perfect day—whether the owners are spending it alone, with their family, or with good friends. The surrounding woods and landscaping create a strong sense of privacy, while a spa cascade emanates a soothing gurgle.

The grilling counter is located just beyond the backdoor for convenience. With the kitchen just steps away, the homeowners opted not to include a sink or refrigerator. They were, however, choosy about their grill. Steaks are a favorite, and they love the way an infrared grill sears the meat to seal in its juices.

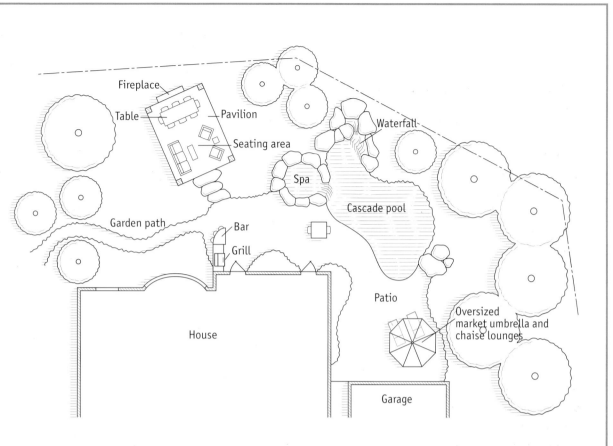

facing page top • The hearth was raised to table height, which improves both its visibility and its heat distribution. Sheer curtains provide the perfect screening to keep out mosquitoes or to soften the light as the sun drops toward the horizon.

facing page bottom • The grilling island is located just beyond the backdoor and features infrared burners for quickly searing meats. Appetizers and drinks are often served here, as friends enjoy hanging out with the chef while dinner sizzles on the grill.

right • In or out of the water, there are plenty of places to relax in this suburban backyard. Evening activities begin at the grilling island, then migrate to the pavilion for a seated dinner, and afterward move to a cushioned seating area.

Configuring the Kitchen Layout

The layout of a kitchen is influenced by several factors: the space itself, the components of the kitchen, traffic patterns, prevailing winds, and personal work preferences. Basic layout options include a single counter; dual counters forming a galley arrangement; and L-shaped, U-shaped, and G-shaped (rectangular or square) configurations. Creative designers have even conceived curving, arched, and circular layouts—though they are generally a variation on one of the basic themes.

Counters may be placed against a house wall, built into a courtyard or retaining wall, positioned along one edge of a patio or deck, or designed as freestanding islands that can be accessed on all sides. Raised bars or table extensions can be added to counter sections for built-in seating to create a space-saving feature that is both practical and popular.

Many outdoor chefs find that a work triangle created between a grill, sink, and work counter is convenient. In reality, not all outdoor kitchens have sinks. And it isn't possible to create a working triangle on a single counter, so work triangles are far less important outdoors than indoors. Instead, focus on creating work zones: a hot zone for grills, burners, and wood-burning ovens; a cold zone for refrigerators, coolers, and ice makers; a wet zone for sinks and beverage centers; and a dry zone for food preparation, plating, and serving. Start by placing the hot zone along one end of a counter or in a far corner for safety and comfort. Cold zones should be placed where it's most convenient to serve beverages. Wet and dry zones may be adjacent to simplify food preparation, though it's very helpful to have at least a little counter space in every zone.

facing page • With its U-shaped configuration, there's enough counter space here for multiple chefs. The broad opening and generous floor space offer plenty of room to move about. Guests fit in, too, owing to the comfortable seating at the bar.

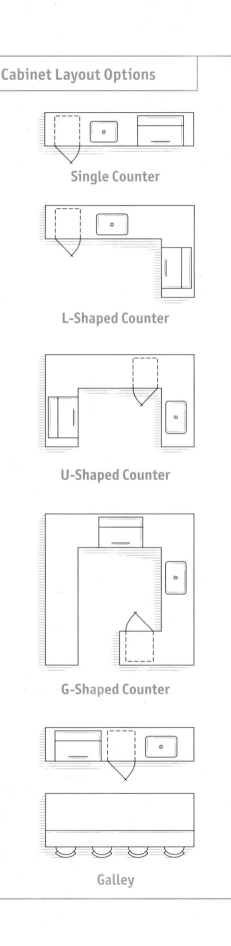

Cabinet Layout Options

Single Counter

L-Shaped Counter

U-Shaped Counter

G-Shaped Counter

Galley

Entertaining a Crowd

Perhaps it's only fitting that the first party ever hosted at this house took place before the home-owners even moved in. A local home and garden magazine was seeking a location for a special event, and the house—with its spectacular views of southern New Mexico's Organ Mountains—was perfect. It's one of those places that simply begs for a party, and this outdoor kitchen island serves as the hub of all festivities.

The island is convenient to the kitchen and indoor storage and has easy access to the driveway—which simplifies matters considerably for catered events when food, beverages, ice, serving pieces, and flowers are delivered. The island itself, just under 13 sq. ft., features nearly 36 ft. of counter space for food preparation and plating, plus a large gas grill, a built-in bar center, and an under-counter refrigerator. And there's enough space inside the island for a chef, bartender, and several assistants to move around. The raised bar, which wraps around the entire island, is almost as popular a gathering place as the adjacent swimming pool, spa, and waterfall.

Though it can handle a crowd, this outdoor kitchen island also works for smaller gatherings. There's room for everyone to pull a stool up to the bar for a casual dinner or to visit with the chef before heading indoors for a more formal dinner. For guests who plan on spending a Saturday around the pool, the refrigerator is a convenient place to store snacks and cold beverages, and the counter makes a good spot for lunch.

right • Pergolas provide a ceiling and place to mount lights. This one features low-maintenance powder-coated steel beams that won't warp or rot and don't have to be repainted. They make a practical alternative to wood beams.

above · Designed for large gatherings, this kitchen island is ideally suited for catered affairs. With nearly 36 ft. of counter space, there's plenty of room to stage food and set up a bar. Extra supplies and containers can be stashed beneath the counters.

left · The base cabinets feature a cultured-stone veneer topped by a 44-in.-high granite-slab bar counter and steel-reinforced cast-concrete columns. The bar has an 11-in. overhang that easily accommodates bar stools.

below · The countertops are made from square granite tiles that match the granite-slab bar. They are set on concrete board, which sits atop a layer of roofing tar that prevents water from seeping into the wood frame.

Addressing Practical Matters

Grills and wood-burning ovens can reach extremely hot temperatures, so creating a safe environment for outdoor entertaining should be a top priority. Begin by locating the grill or oven away from heavily traveled areas or block casual access to it with a run of counters. Also, position it downwind of prevailing breezes and at least 4 ft. away from dining or seating areas to keep the space from getting too hot and to minimize drifting smoke, spattering grease, or sparks. Carefully follow manufacturers' recommendations for installing grills, using fireproof enclosures and cabinet vents to reduce flammability. Also use common sense when positioning any grill, giving it a generous buffer from roofs, trees, or other materials that might melt or catch on fire. If built beneath a roof or overhang, a hood vent may be required.

Most construction projects—including many outdoor kitchens—fall under the jurisdiction of local building codes. Contact local officials to determine whether or not you'll need a building permit and to identify any applicable codes. Although the degree of regulation varies from one community to another, there are almost always codes regarding the installation of any electrical, gas, and plumbing lines, and there may be setback requirements that specify how far any construction must be from the property line. Check with your utility companies as well; they have their own set of guidelines that may be more comprehensive and may override building codes. Remember, these codes have been developed for your safety.

Large grills, wood-burning ovens, and masonry cabinets are heavy. For this reason, they are usually set on a slab of reinforced concrete, which is poured over a bed of gravel. In cold climates, deep footings may be required as well. If building an outdoor kitchen on a deck or porch, have a building inspector check your deck to determine whether or not additional support will be required.

Multiple Outlets Offer Convenience

When planning your outdoor kitchen, don't forget to include multiple electrical outlets. Installing them every few feet along your kitchen cabinet will make it easy to plug in electric grill starters, under-counter refrigerators, blenders, holiday lights, portable radios, fans, and more. For added convenience, also install them on walls and arbor posts.

Remember that all outlets must include a GFCI (ground-fault circuit interrupter) that will protect against shock or electrocution if any electrical product comes in contact with water. Outlet covers should be used to give the outlets protection from the weather, and only extension cords rated for outdoor use should be employed. Also, never leave an extension cord plugged into an outlet unless the other end is plugged into an electrical product.

Although it is often overlooked, multiple natural-gas outlets can also prove convenient. In addition to gas grills, items such as side burners, fireplaces, fire pits, and patio heaters can all be fueled with natural gas.

left · With everything built under the roof of a partially enclosed courtyard pavilion, good ventilation is essential. A commercial-grade hood positioned over the grill's cooking surface keeps the outdoor room free of smoke.

On the Veranda

Porches, porticos, verandas, and piazzas—all forms of covered patios—have a long history in the Deep South, where they've been treated as relaxed outdoor living rooms since pre–Civil War (and pre-air-conditioning) times. Though outdoor kitchens weren't originally part of the equation, they are wonderful modern additions that make these sheltered spaces all the more inviting.

This Charleston-style home has a gracious granite bar that provides seating while screening the working side of an outdoor kitchen. Although the outdoor kitchen and dining areas are used primarily for day-to-day family activities, they were thoughtfully designed to accommodate larger gatherings as well. Double doors open up from the veranda into both a central hallway and the family room, which improves circulation and helps keep individual rooms from getting too crowded. The bar is well equipped, with both a refrigerator and bar center, which make catering to guests' thirst a snap. And as a testament to details that make all the difference: The mounted bottle opener and catch bin are a real time saver and eliminate the need to rummage through drawers for an opener.

The kitchen design, which features a high bar and closed-galley arrangement against a far wall, ensures that the chef and any caterers have plenty of privacy and that any messes created while cooking remain out of view when dinner is served. Even so, the bar, with its comfortable seating, encourages plenty of interaction with the chef while food sizzles on the grill. And on a hot day, you just might find these homeowners serving mint juleps.

above · The stainless-steel natural-gas grill and side burner feature a matching stainless-steel hood for whisking away smoke. It is located safely at the far end of the L-shaped counter, and surrounded by a fire-resistant travertine tile wall.

below · This stainless-steel bar features a bar sink, insulated beverage cooler with sliding cover, four condiment containers (convenient for lemons and limes), a bottle rail (doubling here as a paper-towel holder), a towel rack, and a bottle opener.

above • Clean, classic lines and a simple color scheme help make this space attractive and inviting. The mosaic tile mural serves as a strong focal point on the far wall, while the veranda overlooks a sunken garden and pool.

Drawing Up Your Plans

Sketching rough plans is a good way explore ideas and refine your thinking—even if you're planning to hire a designer. Drawing skills aren't required, but you'll need graph paper, a measuring tape, and a pencil. Measure the boundaries of your designated space, starting with a wall or other existing point in the landscape that can be used for reference. Note any existing features such as patios, paths, trees, and shrubs. Transfer these measurements to graph paper using a ¼-in. scale (¼ in. = 1 ft.), and make several photocopies of this base plan so you can experiment with different ideas without having to redraw the plan each time.

Next, designate areas for cooking, dining, entertaining, and other outdoor activities. Whether you simply draw loose circles indicating these spaces or block them out in more detail doesn't matter. Play with different arrangements of the spaces—consider traffic flow; evaluate space requirements for cabinets, grills, furniture, and other elements; think about how you'll divide the spaces visually; and determine how you might create passageways (real or implied) between them.

Once you are satisfied with the organization of space, you can begin to arrange furniture, cabinets, appliances, and other features within it. Obtain basic measurements (most are available on the manufacturer's website) and make scale cutouts that can be easily arranged on paper. Make sure there is enough space to move about and to pull chairs out from any tables. If you're designing your own outdoor kitchen, you're now ready to move on to detailed plans. If you're working with a professional designer, share these ideas to help him or her gain a better understanding of what you want. And when the designer presents a plan, you will have the advantage of being familiar with the space, its features, and its unique challenges.

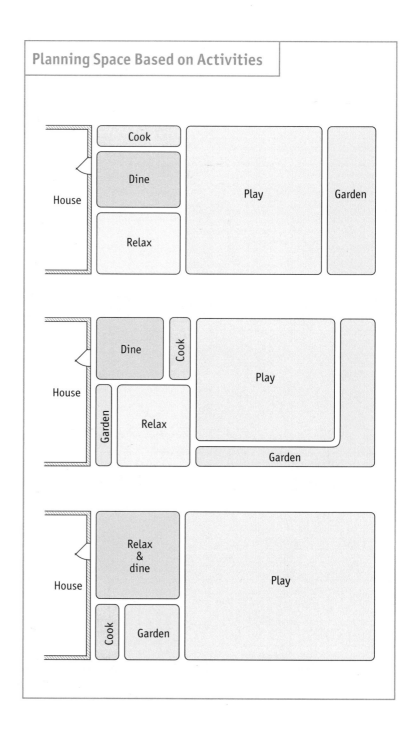

Planning Space Based on Activities

facing page• **When a grill is placed downwind on an open-sided pavilion, it is usually possible to forgo a hood vent. This grill is surrounded by roughly 2 ft. of counter space on either side, which is convenient for cooking and serving.**

Common Measurements

For finished construction drawings, exact measurements are essential. But in the early planning stages, these common footprint measurements can be helpful for roughing out space requirements and playing with potential layouts.

- Grills: 30 in. to 48 in. wide by 24 in. to 36 in. deep
- Bar sink: 15 sq. in.
- Single and double sinks: 20 in. to 32 in. wide by 20 in. deep
- Refrigerator: 24 sq. in.
- Counter depth: 30 in. to 36 in. deep
- Bistro table: 36 in. dia.
- Round table for four: 48 in. dia.
- Rectangular table for six: 68 in. to 72 in. long by 36 in. deep
- Arm chair: 22 in. wide by 24 in. deep
- Side chair: 18 in. wide by 21 in. deep
- Upholstered sofa: 68 in. to 80 in. long by 38 in. deep
- Upholstered casual chair: 28 in. to 32 in. long by 26 in. to 34 in. deep
- Chaise longue: 77 in. long by 26 in. wide
- Coffee table: 36 in. to 46 in. long by 20 in. to 24 in. deep
- Side table: 20 in. to 24 sq. in.

At least 24 in. to 36 in. of counter space on either side of the grill and sink is recommended for plates, tools, and serving. From the edge of a table, allow at least 42 in. on all sides as a comfort zone and for getting in and out of chairs and at least 60 in. from any steps for safety.

GRILLS,

The grill is the heart of the outdoor kitchen—

everything else is secondary.

SMOKERS, AND

You need one that is reliable, is easy to use,

and cooks food the way you like it.

WOOD-BURNING

Grills come in a range of sizes, styles, and budgets,

so you're sure to find one that fits your space and budget.

OVENS

Grills and Smokers

The one piece of equipment that virtually every outdoor kitchen has in common is a grill. It may be a tiny table-top grill, a double-barrel smoker–grill, or a 36-in. gas grill in a grilling island. Thanks to the growing interest in outdoor kitchens, you can now find a quality grill to suit your budget, be it $100, which will get you the most basic type, to thousands of dollars for a top-of-the-line version with all the bells and whistles, such as side burners, rotisseries, woks, and smoker boxes.

There are several basic methods of cooking outdoors—grilling directly over coals, grilling indirectly with the food away from the coals, and smoking foods slowly by infusing them with the heat and fumes of smoldering charcoal and wood. There are also variations on this theme, such as using dual fuels, adding smoke during the grilling process, searing meats with infrared heat, and cooking convection style with pellets. So it's important to think about what you typically like to cook and which methods would be most appropriate before buying a grill.

One of the first decisions you'll need to make is whether you prefer a portable or permanent grill. Portable grills are lighter weight and often come with wheels so that you can move them easily—whether it's from one corner of the patio to another or across town when you buy a new home. Permanent grills come in drop-in or slide-in models that are built into a grilling counter. You may not be able to take them with you when you move, but they will likely enhance the value of your home.

right • Although breezes aren't an issue along this interior portico wall, a hood vent was still essential to keep the area from filling with smoke. By building the cabinet against the wall, easy access was provided to gas, electrical, and water lines.

Grilling Terminology

Direct grilling is a quick-cooking method in which vegetables, seafood, and thin cuts of meat are placed directly over the coals or burner.

Indirect grilling is a slower cooking method in which thick cuts of meat—roasts, ribs, briskets, or whole birds—are placed away from the coals or flame. The lid is kept closed while the food cooks.

Searing is using very high heat to seal in the juices of the meat. This is usually done with the lid open, when the coals or flame are at their hottest. The rest of the cooking can be done at lower temperatures with the lid closed.

Smoking is a slow, indirect cooking process that uses smoldering wood chips to enhance the flavor of foods. A smoky flavor can also be achieved using a pellet grill, the smoker tray on a gas grill, or a foil-wrapped packed of soaked wood chips on a charcoal grill.

above • This portable fire pit is an economical alternative for small spaces and small meals. It burns either wood (best for heating) or charcoal (more convenient for cooking). A full grate is also available for cooking larger meals.

below • Local stone and rustic construction give this hand-built grill character. Broad, removable grates placed at different heights, built-in cabinets and a polished-stone counter offer convenience and flexibility. The Kamado®-style cooker is convenient for smoking meats and grilling small meals.

Grill Types

Most types of grills come in a range of styles, sizes, and finishes. Some are available in a range of fuel options, whereas others are offered only in a single model. All require some sort of protection from the elements—whether a roof overhead or a slip-on vinyl cover.

SMALL PORTABLE GRILL
$
- Easy to move
- Ideal for picnics, tailgating, and small spaces
- Charcoal, gas, and electric models

FREESTANDING GRILL
$–$$
- Easy to move
- Dome, barrel, and flat-topped models
- Wide range of sizes and cooking surfaces
- May feature built-in accessories
- Charcoal, gas, pellet, and electric models

CABINET GRILL
$$–$$$
- Usually easy to move
- Includes storage and workspace
- May feature built-in accessories
- Charcoal and gas models common

SMOKER
$–$$
- Easy to move
- Designed especially for smoking
- May also be used for grilling
- Charcoal and pellet models available

SMOKER–GRILL
$–$$
- Usually easy to move
- Typically two grilling surfaces
- Designed for both smoking and grilling
- Charcoal models only

CUSTOM-BUILT CHARCOAL PIT GRILL

DROP-IN GAS GRILL

CERAMIC COOKERS
$$-$$$
- Easy to move
- Uses hardwood charcoal
- For grilling, smoking, and convection cooking
- Well insulated for moister foods

CUSTOM BUILT
$-$$
- Permanent fixture
- Custom-built to your size and specifications
- No lids—harder to control temperature
- Designed for grilling only
- Charcoal or wood-burning designs common
- Can do it yourself or hire contractor

SLIDE-IN
$$-$$$
- Permanent fixture, slides into island
- Island offers workspace
- Includes built-in storage
- May feature built-in grill accessories
- Charcoal, gas, and pellet models common

DROP-IN
$$-$$$
- Permanent fixture, drops into island
- Island offers workspace and storage
- Does not include built-in storage
- May feature built-in grill accessories
- Charcoal, gas, and pellet models common

BARREL-STYLE CHARCOAL SMOKER–GRILL

SLIDE-IN GAS GRILL

GRILL CONSTRUCTION

The materials grills are made of, which have everything to do with durability, vary more than you might expect. Painted-steel frames and fireboxes are lightweight and economical but must be repainted periodically to prevent rust. Cast aluminum is more expensive but is tough and rust resistant. Stainless steel, which comes in multiple grades, is extremely durable, classic looking, and rust resistant. It should, however, be cleaned periodically, and only the highest grade should be used in seaside conditions. Ceramic is also a durable, low-maintenance housing option used for some smoker–grills.

Cooking grates, or grids, vary in size, material, and design. Those made from porcelain-coated wire or steel are the least expensive, but they may need to be replaced every few years. Cast iron sears food and retains heat well, but must be oiled regularly. Porcelain-coated cast iron solves that problem, but can easily chip and doesn't sear as well. Though less common, anodized aluminum is durable and easy to clean. Stainless steel is the most durable and resists rust, but is more expensive than the other options. As for size, 350 sq. in. to 400 sq. in. is generally suggested as a minimum for most cooks. For large families and those who entertain frequently, 600 sq. in. offers greater flexibility. If you frequently serve large crowds, consider an 800-sq.-in. grate. Grates with wide, closely spaced bars usually sear better than those with narrow, widely spaced bars. Also, adjustable-height grates on charcoal grills offer greater control in cooking.

On gas grills, the burners are the element that must be replaced most often. Most are made from steel, but cast brass, cast iron, and stainless steel are more durable (and more expensive) alternatives. Grills also vary in the number of burners and the power of those burners, which is measured in British Thermal Units (BTUs). More burners offer greater flexibility, especially when cooking multiple dishes. The higher the BTUs, the hotter the flame, but more BTUs aren't necessarily better. Unless you live in a very cold climate where the extra BTUs will allow you to cook faster, they may simply waste fuel. For grills with 350 sq. in. to 600 sq. in. of cooking area, BTU ratings of 35,000 to 50,000 should be adequate.

top • This portable pellet grill features a painted-steel frame and housing that weathers well, but must be touched up with paint from time to time. Sturdy wheels make it easy to move the grill to a screened area when not in use.

above • This drop-in gas grill is constructed from heavy-gauge stainless steel and features a built-in side burner with a cast-iron grate. The cast-iron must be oiled regularly to prevent it from rusting, but it is an excellent conductor of heat.

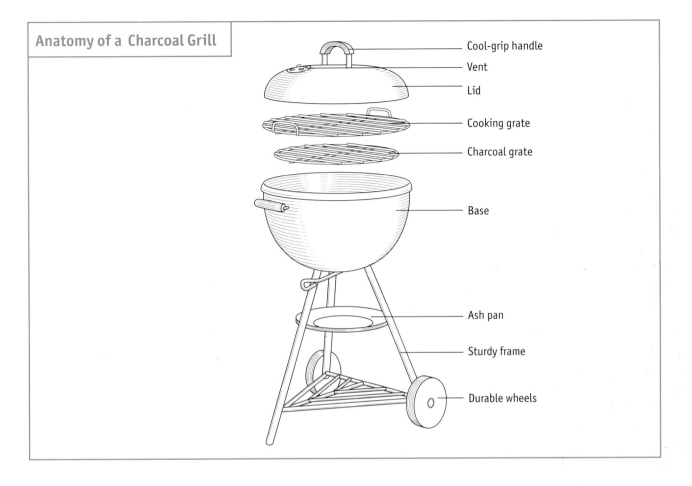

Cool-grip handle

Vent

Lid

Cooking grate

Charcoal grate

Base

Ash pan

Sturdy frame

Durable wheels

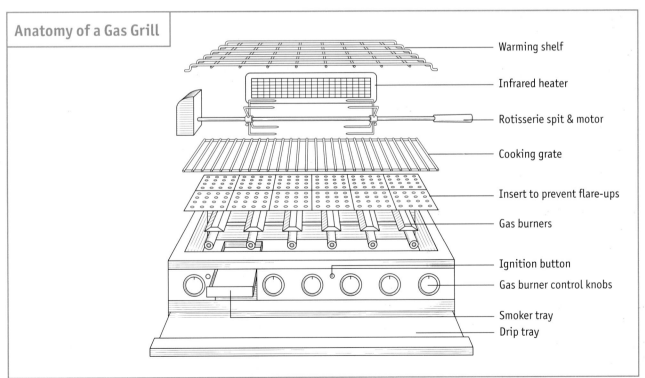

Warming shelf

Infrared heater

Rotisserie spit & motor

Cooking grate

Insert to prevent flare-ups

Gas burners

Ignition button

Gas burner control knobs

Smoker tray

Drip tray

FUEL OPTIONS

As the debate between charcoal and gas continues to rage among grilling enthusiasts, it has also grown in complexity. High-intensity infrared burners and smoker trays on gas grills, gas starters on charcoal grills, and dual-fuel grills now claim to offer the best of all worlds. In addition, wood pellets and electricity offer appealing alternatives to both gas and charcoal.

Charcoal can be messy and takes some time to get hot enough to cook on, but many chefs swear by the flavor it gives meat. Some charcoal aficionados prefer lump hardwood charcoal to traditional charcoal briquettes because it burns hotter and longer; but it is more expensive, harder to find, and harder to light. Gas grills are, by far, the most common type of grill. Though they are more expensive than charcoal grills to install, the fuel costs are lower over the long haul, and ignition systems make lighting them a snap. Electric grills have come a long way: Not only are they perfect for city dwellers who live in tight quarters, but new models rival gas for their ease of use. Pellet grills, with their electric power source and all-natural, renewable fuel, appeal to the environmentally conscious as well as those who enjoy its convenience and smoked-food flavor.

Dual-fuel grills are the new kids on the block. Charcoal grills are available with gas starters that speed up the preheating process. Some pellet grills have gas for searing the meats at higher temperatures than otherwise possible. There are even grills that cook with charcoal, gas, and wood all at the same time.

The three most important factors to consider when it comes to choosing a fuel are what you cook, how much time you have for cooking, and whether or not you like to play with fire. For those who enjoy tinkering with fires, only charcoal will do. If time is of the essence, nothing beats the convenience of gas, infrared, or electric grills. If smoking meats is a specialty, then charcoal or wood pellets may be preferable.

above • This Kamado-style cooker can bake, roast, grill, and smoke foods. It features a heavily insulated housing that helps retain moisture in foods and heat inside the cooker, which makes it especially well suited for slow-cooking techniques.

Pellet Grills

Pellet grills—relative newcomers to the grilling world—are powered by standard, household electrical current (110v). Small wood pellets are fed through an auger, while air from a convection blower helps them combust in the fire pot. The hot wood-fire vapors then surround and cook the food evenly. Controlled by a microprocessor, the auger speed determines the internal temperature of the grill. The pellets are a renewable resource, made from 100% natural hardwood sawdust (no glue or binders are used).

The pellets in this hopper are made from 100 percent hardwood sawdust. Pellets made from apple, oak, mesquite, and other hardwoods are available for infusing foods with different smoked flavors.

left • This gas grill features infrared burners throughout, which quickly reach high temperatures to sear meats, sealing in their juices. They finish cooking the meat and cook other food items at lower temperatures.

below • This tiny grill is made to go. It may not serve a crowd, but it's perfect for two people, a picnic, tailgating, or tight spaces. This one features a butane cylinder as a fuel source.

Fuel Options

Fuel is largely a personal choice based on convenience, flavor, and lifestyle. Location sometimes figures into the equation as well—as natural gas, electric, and electricity-driven pellet grills require access to utilities.

CHARCOAL
- Briquettes and natural lump hardwood
- Gives food a distinct smoky flavor
- Easily sears meat to seal in juices
- Cooks hotter than most other grills
- Takes time to prepare fire
- Difficult to control temperature and maintain extended fire

GAS
- Liquid propane tanks or as natural gas lines
- Lights quickly
- Offers greater control over temperatures than charcoal
- Does not burn as hot as charcoal
- Multiple burners offer flexibility
- Burns for a long time without refueling
- Doesn't impart a flavor

WOOD LOGS
- Used in wood-burning ovens and camp-style fire pits
- More difficult to light than charcoal
- Takes longer to reach cooking temperature than other types
- Challenging to control temperature
- Gives food a smoky flavor

WOOD PELLETS
- Made from 100% pure hardwood sawdust
- Convection airflow cooks food evenly without turning
- Gives food a smoky flavor
- Flavored wood pellets available
- Offers multirange temperature control
- Generates a lot of smoke when first started

ELECTRIC
- Easy to start, but slow to heat up
- Easy to control heat
- Lacks smoky flavor
- Ideal in locations where smoke would be a problem

NATURAL GAS

LIQUID PROPANE

SHOPPING FOR A GRILL

If you haven't shopped for a grill in a while, you may be surprised, if not overwhelmed, by the variety of brands, models, features, and configurations available. Before heading to the store, it helps to know the following:

- **What You'll Probably Cook Most Often.** That way, you won't be tempted by accessories you don't need.

- **Your Fuel Preference.** Consider what you cook, how much time you have to cook, and whether you enjoy building a fire.

- **How Many People You'll Cook for on a Regular Basis.** The grill surface should be just large enough to cook everyone's food at the same time. If you do much indirect grilling or cook an entire meal on the grill, allow more space.

- **How Often You Plan to Grill.** Choose a grill that won't wear out after just a few years of use.

- **How Much Space Is Available.** This is especially important if your patio, porch, or deck is small.

- **Your Budget.** Grill prices vary by thousands of dollars. While lifespan or durability is a key cost factor, it's often size, power, and add-on features that run up the price. It's possible to find a solid, functional grill in every price range.

Once you've narrowed your choices to a few grills in your price range, give each a good shake. It should feel sturdy and solid, and the wheels should roll easily. Lift the lid: It shouldn't be too heavy or awkward. Check the grates and any burners to make sure they're made of durable materials that won't rust. Look for safety features, such as cool-touch handles and metal or ceramic inserts on gas grills that prevent flare-ups. Check the ash pans on charcoal grills and drip pans on gas grills: They should be deep and easily accessible for cleanup. Make sure controls on gas grills are easy to read and operate, and look for both top and bottom vents on charcoal grills for the greatest control over temperatures. Compare special features to make sure you're not buying more than you need. And finally, don't forget to read the warranty. It should be straightforward and from a company you trust.

top • This professional-grade grill is both good looking and extremely well built. It features heavy-gauge stainless-steel housing, stainless-steel grates, brass burners, a dual-position rotisserie, a rear infrared burner, and a built-in temperature gauge.

above • This built-in temperature gauge shows temperature ranges for warming, smoking, and grilling foods rather than actual temperatures—a great tool for indicating when the grill has reached, and is maintaining, an appropriate temperature for a particular task.

facing page bottom • This sleekly designed grilling cart features a pull-out drawer for utensils; a cabinet for storing cleaning tools and screening the propane tank from view; a side shelf for plates; and a side burner that, when covered, doubles as another work shelf.

Handy Accessory Holder

When grilling, you need your tools at hand—not back in the kitchen or sitting on the deck railing. Many grills come with a shelf for setting down a plate, but too few offer hooks for hanging spatulas, forks, and hot mitts. This ingenious kettle grill design not only has small shelves but also has plenty of hooks for utensils and even an enclosed lower shelf just large enough for a small bag of charcoal or grill-cleaning tools.

A Versatile Outdoor Kitchen — Grill, Bake, or Smoke

Whether it's a quick weekday dinner on the grill, pizza with the Girl Scout troop, burgers for an afternoon around the pool, or smoked delicacies for a philanthropic gathering, this outdoor kitchen gets used on a regular basis. The homeowners are good-natured entertainers who host fund-raising events for a variety of social and environmental causes. Rather than throw the usual formal affair, they prefer entertaining in a more relaxed outdoor setting on this side-yard patio and around the backyard pool—a change of pace welcomed by partygoers.

Because it is quick and easy, the gas grill and bar (located at the end of the curved grilling island) are perfect for weekday lunches and family dinners. The pizza oven and smoker—a Kamado-style cooker that burns lump hardwood charcoal—take a little longer to fire up, so they are used more often when entertaining friends and hosting events or when pool parties are in full swing.

The unique curved grilling island was designed to mimic the curvilinear layout of the terrace, which followed the natural grade of the landscape. It was also designed to keep the appliances and storage units behind the island where they would be screened from view, which leaves the patio looking crisp and tidy rather than cluttered. Although it was a bit challenging fitting square appliances into a curved cabinet, the builder elongated the curve at specific points to eliminate any protruding appliance corners. The bar area was oriented so the diners could visit face-to-face with the chef while meals are being cooked and to and enjoy the sweeping view over the treetops.

above · **This wood-burning oven features a modular oven insert and custom exterior finish. It is built at a comfortable working height, as pizzas and breads are moved in and out of the oven from a standing position on long-handled paddles.**

above • The curving patio wall responds to the natural lay of the land. Likewise, the curvilinear grilling island echoes the curves of the patio wall. The same stucco finish was used on the wall, cabinet base, and wood-burning oven to create a sense of unity.

below • The refrigerator, sink, grill, and warming drawer are all accessed from the rear of this grilling island. The result is a sleek, contemporary look for the patio and a private (yet not isolated) workspace for the chef.

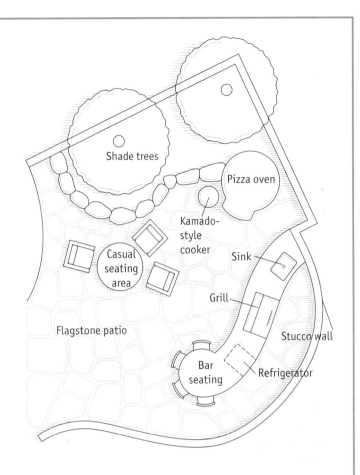

Shade trees

Pizza oven

Kamado-style cooker

Casual seating area

Sink

Grill

Flagstone patio

Stucco wall

Bar seating

Refrigerator

Side Burners

Side burners are a lot like the burners on a kitchen stove and are used in a similar fashion. They are perfect for heating sauces, steaming vegetables, warming soups, and preparing other side dishes that aren't cooked on the grill. They are commonly sold as one- or two-burner units, and may include a wok station, griddle, or cooking grid. Some even feature a built-in chopping board for convenience. All should be covered when not in use to protect the burners.

Side burners are most often available as drop-in units for grilling islands. However, many portable gas grills—especially those with built-in carts—now feature side burners. Also some side burners can be purchased with a separate, freestanding stainless-steel cabinet. For those with charcoal and pellet grills or portable gas grills without a side burner there are small, portable side burners that operate with butane or propane cylinders. Look for them where camping or catering supplies are sold.

For more serious off-grill cooking—such as a fish fry, turkey fry, or low-country boil—a separate higher-powered, low-pressure burner is called for. Often sold as "turkey fryers," "fish cookers," or "professional cookers," at hardware stores, these burners feature a large cooking surface that supports oversize pots for boiling, steaming, deep-frying, or stewing meals. They come in one-, two-, or three-burner units and connect to liquid propane tanks.

top · This double side burn features a drop-in maple cutting board and a deep utility drawer for oversize cooking utensils. The bar-grate design accommodates a griddle plate, which is perfect for cooking up a breakfast of bacon, eggs, and pancakes.

right · Setting this portable propane-tank burner directly on the patio floor makes it easier to work with oversize pots of boiling water or deep-frying oil safely. However, it must be used with extreme caution (or not at all) when young children are present.

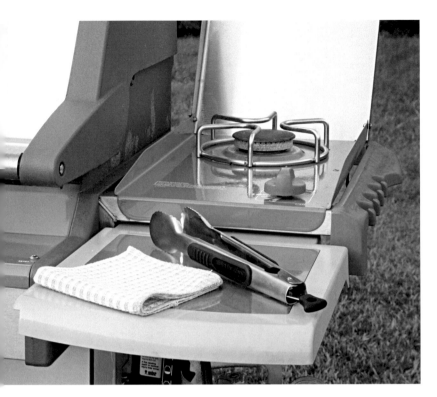

above left · This single-burner unit is a feature on a freestanding portable grill and is fueled by liquid propane. The attached flip top offers a convenient way to remove the lid without having to find a place to put it.

above right · A push-button ignition (to left of temperature control knob) makes starting this single side burner a snap. Foods can be boiled, simmered, or heated in frying pans, saucepans, or small stockpots just as they are on a kitchen stove.

left · An economical alternative to heavier-duty stainless-steel side burners, this portable butane burner is a practical solution for travel, outdoor kitchens without a gas grill, and cooking areas located away from the house.

Grill Accessories

Today's grills, with their many accessories, are for more than just grilling. Rotisseries with a motor and rotating spit can be added to gas grills for roasting and barbecuing meats. Because the spits are frequently positioned a considerable distance from the burners, infrared panels are often placed behind the rotisserie to cook the meat more quickly and evenly. Infrared burners are also sometimes placed among the standard gas burners to create a searing zone in the grill. Smoking trays and boxes that hold wood chips are also features on many gas grills. They allow foods to be flavored with alder, apple, mesquite, oak, pecan, or other wood chips.

Many grills come with a warming shelf—a narrow grate at the back of the grill, above the cooking surface—for heating buns and breads, or keeping foods warm before they are served. Warming drawers, which are sold separately from the grill, also serve this purpose. They hold larger quantities of food (as well as plates) out of the way of the grill. Look for multiple racks, temperature controls, moisture controls, automatic shut-off features, and easy-glide drawers.

Grills of all types frequently come with a thermometer built into the hood. This measures the temperature of the grill (rather than the food), so that the heat level can be adjusted as necessary—whether that means turning a knob, switching an auger into higher gear, or adding more coals to the fire. Another built-in convenience is a lamp that sheds light on the cooking surface. Look for an adjustable type built on the side of the grill or a light built into the lid. Lights can also be built into hood vents, an important accessory for grills built beneath an overhang.

top right · With temperature settings from 90 degrees to 250 degrees, this warming oven can be used for heating plates, warming breads, or keeping soups and sauces hot. It also features a moisture-control selector that helps keep foods crisp or moist.

right · An adjustable burner is built in beneath the smoker tray in this gas grill, making it easier to control the amount of smoke produced by smoldering wood chips or wood chunks. Soaking the chips first will keep them from burning too quickly.

Infrared Burners

Infrared is a form of radiant energy—not unlike visible light, radio waves, and microwaves—that can cook foods quickly without drying them out the way other fuels can. Infrared heats to extremely high temperatures (as much as 2,000 degrees) for searing meats, and it does so much more quickly (in as little as 3 minutes to 5 minutes on some units) than other grills. It also cooks foods as much as 50 percent faster than gas, charcoal, or electricity. Because drippings are instantly vaporized, there are also fewer flare-ups. Many higher-end gas grills are equipped with infrared burners for searing meats or adjacent to the rotisserie for more even cooking. In some cases, grills are equipped with infrared on all burners.

This infrared burner replaces a standard burner, making it possible to sear meats at a very high temperature in a gas grill.

left · It helps if you can see what you're cooking. This light is mounted to the grill base and sports a flexible stand. Hood lights, clip-on lamps, and overhead task lights work equally well to illuminate the cooking surface after dark.

Hood Vents

Although most outdoor kitchens don't require hood vents, they are essential for whisking away smoke when grills are located beneath covered areas such as porches, porticos, pavilions, or pool houses. Because they have to compete with wind, more-powerful commercial-grade units are most effective, and they should be positioned out from the wall so that they are directly over the cooking surface.

1. This stainless-steel hood vent is recessed in traditional kitchen cabinetry (well protected by a deep portico), creating an overall look that almost fools you into thinking this is an indoor kitchen. 2. With its stucco and tile exterior, this recessed hood blends almost seamlessly with the backsplash and surrounding walls rather than matching the grill. 3. This hood is completely enclosed and hidden from view because the entire grilling cabinet was recessed into the side of a house wall (occupying space that might otherwise be used as a closet). 4. Rather than recess or downplay the hood, the designer turned this hood into a dominant architectural element of the outdoor kitchen. 5. Big grills require big hoods. This commercial-kitchen-styled grill with backsplash and hood is used often for hosting large parties.

Grilling Tools

In addition to accessories for the grill, there are an unlimited number of tools for the avid griller. Some, like fire-retardant mitts and long-handled utensils (forks, spatulas, knives, and tongs), make grilling safer. Others, such as electric charcoal starters, charcoal chimneys, and meat thermometers, make the task at hand a little easier.

The broadest and fastest-growing category of grilling tools is cookware. These pots, pans, and baskets make it possible to cook foods on the grill that you might not ordinarily consider, or at least to cook certain foods more easily. The most useful of these gadgets are those that keep food from falling through the cracks on the grate or allow you to cook foods that would simply be too messy otherwise. Long-handled fish baskets let you flip fish without it falling apart. Grill-top vegetable baskets are great for tossing veggies without worry. Griddles let you start your day with bacon, eggs, and pancakes from the grill. A cast-iron wok makes it possible to stir-fry just about anything. Cedar planks not only provide a solid cooking surface, but they also infuse the food with flavor as it cooks. Roasting pans, rib racks, pizza stones, Dutch ovens, upright poultry roasters, skewers, and grill presses are just a few of the other cookware items that have been redesigned for outdoor use.

As for other types of tools, some make cleanup easier (or at least a little neater): grate brushes, stainless-steel cleaner, and even Grill Floss™—a gadget that cuts through caked-on grate gunk in those hard to reach places. A few tools for the griller could be considered quite fashionable—stylish aprons and tall chef's hats are among them. Others aren't so much tools as they are specialty food items: Witness the explosion of sauces, seasonings, and rubs now available for spicing up grilled foods. And for the chef who has it all, how about a hand-forged, monogrammed branding iron for personalizing steaks?

above • Forget the lighter fluid. A charcoal chimney starter is easier and safer to use, and won't infuse your food with faint hints of petroleum. Just place paper in the bottom, pour charcoal in the top, and light your match.

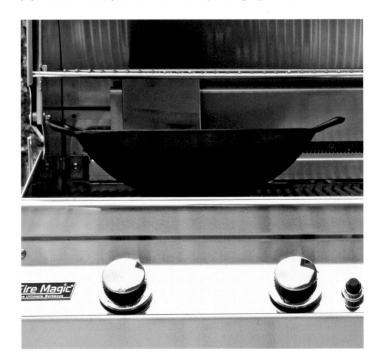

right • Cast-iron absorbs and retains heat at the high temperatures required for stir-frying foods. This flat-bottomed wok was designed for use on a grill or stove. It is heavy, but can be easily lifted with two hot pads or grilling mitts.

above • If a pizza oven isn't in the cards, this specially designed baking stone will turn an ordinary grill into a pizza grill. The porous clay stone produces a pizza with a crisp crust and bubbly toppings.

above • These kiln-dried cedar planks (also available in alder) can be used several times for grilling fish over a low fire. Afterward, they can be cut into chunks for smoking meats. Either way, they infuse salmon and other fish with a wonderful, smoky flavor.

right • This griddle is perfect for cooking up a plate of sausage and pancakes. The turned-up edges will keep the pancake batter from running onto the grill before it's had time to set.

Grill Safety

Grills—not just the coals and burners, but the firebox and lid—reach extremely high temperatures. A few commonsense precautions can help ensure that your backyard barbecue doesn't go up in flames.

Place grills at least 15 in. from flammable surfaces such as wood siding, tree branches, or awnings. Inspect propane tanks and natural gas lines regularly for cracks or corrosion that could lead to dangerous gas leaks. Avoid disposing of spent charcoal and wood ashes until they are completely cool. And use paper or kindling rather than lighter fluid to revive a charcoal or wood fire to prevent flare-ups.

If a fire does flare up, close the grill lid to suffocate most of the flames. For a grease fire, douse it with baking soda. Never throw water on a grease fire, however, as water can cause the grease to spatter and spread. And always keep a fire extinguisher nearby for emergencies.

above • Digital meat thermometers with probes now come with wireless remotes. If you're away from the grill tending to other chores or visiting with guests, they can be programmed to beep when the food is done.

below • Long-handled tools are essential when cooking over hot fires. These are made from stainless steel with cool-to-touch, wooden handles. The long mitt is not only padded but fire retardant as well.

Wood-Burning Ovens

As practical as they are beautiful, wood-burning masonry ovens (also called clay bake ovens or brick ovens) have been used for centuries to bake great-tasting bread and crisp-crust pizza. Less well known, they can also be used to roast whole turkeys and other meats, as well as to bake fish, potatoes, beans, soups, and stews in stainless-steel, cast-iron, and terra-cotta pots. It's even possible to grill steaks, hamburgers, chicken breasts, and pork chops inside a wood-burning oven.

What makes a wood-burning oven unique is the cooking environment—a combination of conductive heat from the cooking surface, reflective heat from the dome, and convection heat from the hot air circulating throughout the oven. For this reason, there are different techniques for cooking in wood-burning ovens. Pizza, for instance, is cooked quickly at a very high temperature. The fire is simply moved to one side of the oven and the door is left open while the pizza quickly bakes. Grilling is also done over a hot fire: A specially designed grate is placed over wood coals and the oven door is left open while meats cook. Once the high-heat cooking has been finished, the fire is removed and the door is closed. This retains an appropriate amount of heat for baking breads and roasting meats. As the oven cools further, pots of soups, stews, and beans can slowly simmer until they reach perfection. Some people even keep foods inside the oven overnight for the next day's meals.

top • Decorative touches like these tiles and river cobbles enhance the design of a pizza oven and help tie it visually to the home or landscape. This pizza oven also has a thick, poured concrete shelf built in for plates, tools, and drink glasses.

above • Technically speaking, the wood-burning oven is just the insulated, domed insert and not the stand or physical surrounds. Once this oven was set, these creative homeowners turned the surrounds into something quite fanciful.

Long-handled tools are kept near the oven for convenience:
large peels for handling pizza and bread, smaller utility peels
for shifting pizzas or moving pots inside the oven, ash shovels
for removing the fire, and brushes for cleaning the oven floor.

above • The design of this large wood-burning oven is based on the traditional horno, or bread oven, found throughout America's desert Southwest. It serves as a focal point on the patio and is in scale with the heavy beams above the outdoor kitchen.

Pizza Oven As a Small-Space Solution

While this house is positioned to enjoy stunning views of the surrounding Sonoma Valley countryside, it was built very close to the rear property line. This left only a narrow space for a deck and outdoor kitchen. The deck runs more than half the length of the house with a seating area for two and dining table that seats four to six. An indoor room extends to the edge of the deck along a quarter of the house. And that leaves just enough space for a wood-burning oven and podium-size stand-up counter on the ground level next to the deck. This triangular-shaped counter is just the right size for a plate of appetizers and a couple of drinks—enabling the chef to socialize while he's tending the fire and cooking the meal. A small, concrete shelf extends from the oven itself, providing a place to park utensils as well as food coming and going from the oven.

above • The arbor, which is constructed from pressure-treated lumber and copper pipes, frames the cooking area, making it feel like an outdoor room with high ceilings and grand picture windows even though it is a fairly small space.

left • The triangular counter fits the space and is perfectly suited to stand-up entertaining near the pizza oven. Since wood-burning fires take some tending, the counter is much appreciated by the chef and guests.

OVEN CONSTRUCTION

Wood-burning ovens have a rich history that dates back to Roman times. Though much more common in Europe than the United States, they have been built in this country since colonial times. Wood-burning ovens are traditionally made from brick—a time-consuming process mastered by artisans. However, newer models are constructed from high-tech refractory materials that heat up faster, hold heat longer, and are more durable than before. Some argue that a traditional brick oven is a superior cooking environment, but refractory ovens are more affordable and produce excellent results.

Most refractory ovens are shipped in modular parts, which must then be assembled on site and finished with brick, stone, stucco, or tile. They can be assembled by most masons, as well as by homeowners with basic masonry skills. A few models can even be delivered fully built from the factory, ready to set on a stand. But be forewarned: These fully assembled ovens are heavy and must be moved by a forklift or crane.

Another form of wood-burning oven is the horno, or adobe bread oven, which is often seen in the desert southwest. These are made from sun-dried mud bricks that are bonded together with mud mortar. They are rarely seen elsewhere, because the adobe bricks are formed from soil that is unique to this region.

Most wood-burning ovens are set atop stands so that the fires can be maintained and cooking can be done from a comfortable standing position. Though a stand can have a solid face, it is most often left open so that it can be used to store wood conveniently.

right • This pizza oven was built into a retaining wall. In the true spirit of recycling, the wall's boulders had been cleared from the site when the home was built. Wood is kept in nearby dry-storage cabinets.

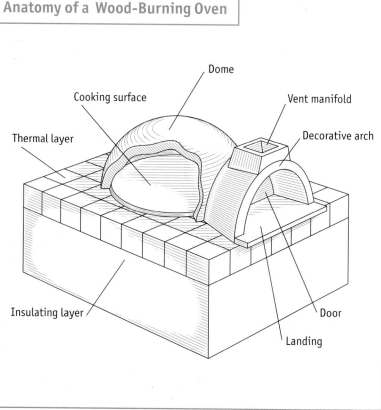

Anatomy of a Wood-Burning Oven

Dome

Cooking surface

Vent manifold

Thermal layer

Decorative arch

Insulating layer

Door

Landing

above • This traditional brick oven, which takes approximately 1 hour to heat for baking, was built along one leg of an L-shaped cabinet to create an outdoor kitchen. A charcoal grill stands at the ready for nights when a quicker meal is necessary.

CABINETS,

Above all else, cabinets, counters, and outdoor appliances must

be durable. They've got to weather whatever Mother Nature

COUNTERS, AND

dishes out—sun, rain, snow, ice, hail, or falling branches—

as well as the daily abuses our families put them through.

APPLIANCES

Design for Function

Outdoor kitchens are different from indoor kitchens in that the basic tools needed to get the job done can vary dramatically from one backyard to another. Sinks and refrigerators—both essential indoors—are immensely useful but entirely optional outdoors. Depending on where food preparation, plating, and serving are handled, an outdoor kitchen may function fine with counter space only 12 in. long or may require more than 12 ft. to be efficient. Outdoor kitchens may need lots of storage, or they might not need any at all. The bottom line is that not all outdoor kitchens are fully equipped. Only you can decide what's important in your kitchen, and it's critical that you make these kinds of decisions early in the process—before you begin buying appliances or designing cabinetry.

When laying out cabinets and appliances, it's helpful to think of hot, cold, wet, and dry zones (see "Designing a Kitchen That Works," beginning on p. 28). But even before you do that, it's important to think in terms of activities: food preparation, cooking, beverage service, food service, eating, cleanup, and storage. In other words, rather than thinking about what you *need*, start by concentrating on what you'll *do* in your outdoor kitchen. Think through a meal—from the storage of raw food to cleanup. If all you're planning to do outside is grill dinner, then a portable grill or small grilling island may be all you need. But if you're planning to prepare your dinner outdoors, it's worth considering a sink, under-counter refrigerator, and ample counter space.

Once you decide what you'll do in your outdoor kitchen, you will know what tools you'll need to get the job done. And once those tools have been selected, you can fit all of the pieces together with cabinets and counters. Throughout this planning process, be sensitive to those tiny details that might be easily overlooked. Utensil hooks, towel racks, and covered storage for trash and recycling bins can be just as important as selecting the right sink or refrigerator.

above • Portable cabinets can work just as hard as built-in cabinets. This homemade potting bench features a built-in sink that is connected to a garden hose, along with plenty of counter and shelf space.

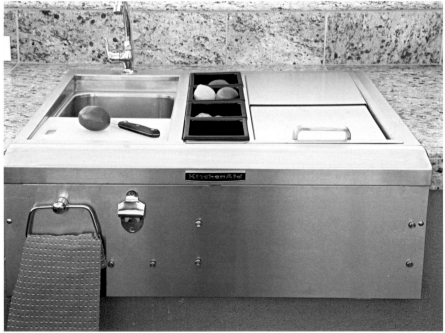

above • With a grill, under-counter refrigerator, drop-in beverage cooler, and ample counter space, this outdoor kitchen is ready for a party. The L-shaped design conveniently faces both the pool deck and a dining pavilion.

left • Bar centers are available in various configurations and are designed to drop into a counter as a single unit. This one features a removable cutting board that's great for slicing fruits and vegetables.

FOOD PREPARATION AND COOKING

It's joy to wash and prepare foods outdoors, especially if some of the herbs, fruits, or vegetables were grown in your own garden. But even if all of the ingredients came from the local market, you can spend more time enjoying the outdoors by chopping your vegetables, assembling your salads, cooking your sauces, and seasoning your meats in an outdoor kitchen.

To do this, you'll need a counter that's nontoxic, easy to clean, and won't stain easily. Otherwise, find a generous cutting board for outdoor food preparation. You'll want plenty of working room, too—at least 12 in. on either side of the sink, though a 2-ft. or 3-ft. run will prove more functional. Allow extra counter space if there will be more than one cook in your outdoor kitchen or if you anticipate using food processors, blenders, mixers, or other countertop appliances. Easily accessible GFCI (ground-fault circuit interrupter) electrical outlets are a must, and task lighting is invaluable as the sun begins to dip in the sky.

A sink makes it easy to wash fruits and vegetables, fill pots for boiling water, rinse your hands and utensils, and clean the counters when done. A drawer for storing utensils and extra towels could come in handy, and a conveniently located trash can is almost always essential. A small bucket for hauling fruit and vegetable scraps to the compost bin is also beneficial.

It's important to remember that the temperatures outside can be much hotter than indoors, especially in summertime. And many foods can attract flying insects if left outdoors on a counter for too long. To keep perishable foods safe and clean, an under-counter refrigerator is ideal for short-term cold storage.

top right • Displaying a beautifully aged patina, this copper sink and faucet blend well into a landscape setting, demonstrating why copper has long been a favorite outdoor building material. The sink is used for cleaning cooking utensils and washing hands as well as rinsing fresh salad greens from the garden.

right • It's almost impossible to have too many GFCI outlets in an outdoor kitchen. This wooden cabinet has one every few feet, located just inches below the counter where they can be easily reached to plug in portable appliances.

above • Some outdoor counters clean up more easily than others; and certain metal surfaces, such as this galvanized sheet metal counter, may contain small quantities of toxins. For these reasons, it's good idea to use a sanitized cutting board for outdoor food preparation.

left • Though the sink may not be very broad, it features a slightly offset, long-necked faucet that simplifies filling up pitchers, rinsing a colander of berries, or scrubbing a small serving platter.

Adapting Commercial Kitchen Equipment

As an avid outdoorsman and cook, this homeowner naturally enjoys entertaining outdoors with his wife and two young daughters. There's plenty of room for the girls to run around in the backyard with their friends while all the parents gather on the patio.

When the family first moved into this home, the homeowner contemplated building a full outdoor kitchen on the patio. About that same time, however, he began working in the family's food-service equipment business. Surrounded by commercial kitchen equipment, he was inspired to bring home a used stainless-steel sink and prep table one day. At first, he thought the sink (which was easily hooked up to a garden hose with an adapter) would be overkill, but found he used it continuously to rinse his hands, utensils, and chopping board as well as to wash fresh-picked vegetables from his garden. Not only did he love the convenience and good looks of his new portable outdoor kitchen, but he started looking around the store for other items that were suited for outdoor use. Long-handled mitts and tools looked like they were made especially for grilling; oversize stainless-steel bowls were perfect for tossing big salads and marinating a dozen chicken breasts at a time; and large stew pots were just right for low-country boils. Portable burners let him prepare side dishes and fry turkeys outdoors.

Among his more surprising finds were colorful melamine school plates and matching red cups, along with the rubber tub sized just right for carrying dirty dishes back indoors for cleanup after a meal. The next time he throws a big party, he's planning to bring home the margarita machine; and the double grill the business rents to caterers will be perfect for grilling quesadillas for a crowd.

top • These rectangular "school plates" are colorful, economically priced, and tough as nails. They're perfect for outdoors—especially when there are lots of children around.

above • It's a long way back to the kitchen, but this rubber tub reduces the number of trips made with dirty dishes. Designed for restaurants and school kitchens, the tubs come in several different sizes.

above • Everything is portable on this patio—even the outdoor kitchen and fire pit. That way, things can be rearranged depending on whether the event is a family dinner, a birthday party for the girls, or entertaining 50 or more friends.

left • The stainless-steel sinks and worktables used in restaurants are extremely durable and are often sold as used equipment when a restaurant closes, moves, or expands. These came from the local food-service equipment dealer.

SERVING, DINING, AND CLEANUP

If you carry platters of food straight from the grill to the table, space requirements for food service may be minimal—just enough counter space to set down those platters when pulling food off the grill. Serving up individual plates requires more space. Of course, outdoor kitchen counters can also serve as buffet counters or double as seating areas. Oversize counters or counter extensions are useful for this purpose—perhaps an island with a counter overhang deep enough to accommodate stools, a separate bump-up counter for raised-bar seating, or even a separate tabletop counter extension.

Beverage service comes with different sets of needs. These can be as simple as storing canned drinks in an under-counter refrigerator or portable cooler or setting a pitcher of drinks and glasses on a counter top. Full bar service for a party requires counter space and greatly benefits from the convenience of a sink. Other appliances that may prove useful are a dedicated wine cooler, an ice maker, a beer tap, and a consolidated bar center containing a small sink, built-in ice cooler, condiment containers, and speed rail for bottles.

For sanitary reasons, most homeowners still store their dishes indoors, and that's where most dishwashing takes place as well. Dishwashers would be a practical consideration for outdoor kitchens located in a pavilion or pool house that can be easily closed up to keep dust to a minimum. But even if the dishwashing is done indoors, it's nice to have a sink for rinsing dishes or platters before they are carried back to the house and for cleaning counters and dining areas. Restaurant-style bins for hauling dishes can help save trips to the kitchen. Trash receptacles are a must, and recycle bins for drink bottles and cans come in handy. Under-counter storage for these items will keep your outdoor kitchen looking neat and will help keep critters away if the trash is left out overnight.

right • A drop-in cooler is a convenient way to serve ice-cold beverages. This one comes with a removable condiment tray and has a drain for melting ice. A sealed lid helps maintain cool temperatures when closed.

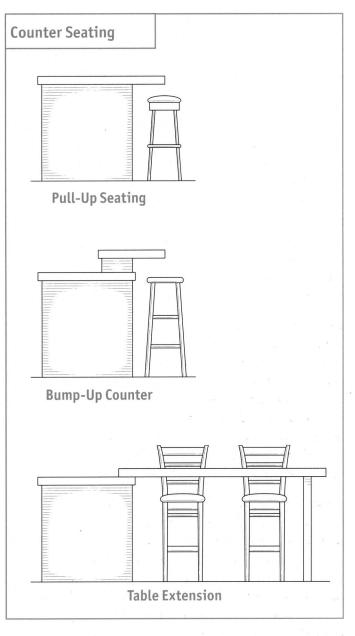

Pull-Up Seating

Bump-Up Counter

Table Extension

facing page top • Generous stretches of counter make an outdoor kitchen more versatile. This 4-ft. counter section can be used for food prep or plating dinners, to serve appetizers and drinks, or as a buffet counter.

left • Every outdoor kitchen needs a trash bin—whether it's a sleek stainless-steel can like this one, a plastic can under the sink, or a hanging bag on the inside of a cabinet door. Choose a location during the planning process so the trash receptacle won't get in your way.

Bars and Carts

For those who prefer portable fixtures to built-in, there are a world of choices in bars, carts, and tables for outdoor use. Furniture stores, home centers, garden supply catalogs, and commercial kitchen shops are all excellent places to look for ideas. In addition to commercially available furnishings, you can build your own or adapt unique finds from antiques stores, yard sales, and flea markets. In fact, the choices are really limited only by your imagination.

1. A small portable bar provides a place to hang out just about anywhere and is perfect for serving drinks during a party. 2. Small rolling carts come in many styles and can be put to many uses. 3. This wooden box opens up into a portable outdoor kitchen for small spaces. When closed, it serves as storage for the cooking gear. 4. Ready-made bars on wheels are portable and party ready. 5. Hand-built or antique tables can be equipped with an old sink for a unique and affordable work surface.

STORAGE

Because temperatures are often much hotter or colder outdoors than in, humidity levels are often elevated, and hungry critters abound, there's little call for food-storage pantries in outdoor kitchens. There are, nonetheless, myriad cold and dry storage needs for items such as:

- Canned and bottled beverages

- Seasonings, sauces, salad dressings, and other bottled condiments

- Grilling, serving, and eating utensils

- Kitchen towels, hot pads, and mitts

- Small appliances such as blenders, food processors, and radios

- Nonbreakable cups, plates, and tableware

- Fuel—charcoal, propane tanks, or wood

- Grill and general cleaning supplies

- Market umbrellas and furniture cushions

- Lanterns, candles, and other tabletop accessories

- Paper goods (best kept in airtight containers)

- Trash and recycling bins

- Outdoor gear, such as pool and gardening supplies

Outdoor cabinetry can be equipped with a variety of cabinets, drawers, and tilt-out panels. If your kitchen backs a wall, overhead wall-hung cabinets are a great solution for storing kitchenware. Many grilling carts offer storage that can be used for fuel tanks, cleaning supplies, and utensils. Furniture designed for outdoor living may include drawers or cabinets. Nearby closets—perhaps in a garage or pool house—can be adapted for outdoor kitchen storage. And a variety of bins, boxes, baskets, racks, shelves, and hooks can be put to good use in and around any outdoor kitchen.

top · **This series of four shallow drawers makes it easier to find all the small things you need outdoors—grilling tools, matches, scissors, and bottle openers—than would two deep drawers. It's simple to remove the drawers for periodic cleaning.**

above · **This wicker hamper is used for storing seat cushions and pillows, but it would work equally well for storing serving baskets, table lanterns, or backyard toys. Hampers are also available in teak and cedar models.**

facing page top · **Inside this garden pavilion, a mix of open shelving, glass-front cabinets, and solid cabinets keep gear in and out of sight, as appropriate. The rear cabinets and shelves are just deep enough for a set of plates or portable appliances.**

Faux Woodpile Door

Pizza ovens burn wood fuel, so storage areas for firewood are often built directly beneath the pizza oven or nearby for convenience. While a neat stack of wood looks great, wood rarely remains neatly stacked. Scrap paper (for starting the fire), tools, lighters, and other items often find their way into this cavity (not to mention an occasional stray critter). This woodpile was kept dry and concealed without losing that nice stacked-wood effect by attaching a faux-woodpile veneer—thinly cut rounds from log ends—to a solid door.

A Kitchen with Abundant Storage

This outdoor kitchen sits on a terraced patio overlooking a swimming pool and spa. Designed as much for growing children as for adults, this outdoor living and recreational area is used for a combination of weeknight dinners, casual family gatherings, children's pool parties, and dinner parties for the adults. The owner wanted to keep nonbreakable tableware, paper goods, and a large supply of beverages in the outdoor kitchen during peak pool season and also needed a place to stash pool toys when not in use. So ample storage was a key design goal when planning this outdoor kitchen.

The owner, a landscape designer, collaborated with a design/build firm that specializes exclusively in outdoor kitchens. The grilling island is a unique I-shaped design that offers multipurpose spaces. The grill and side burner are isolated on the far end, safely away from poolside activities. The opposite end is raised slightly to serve as a stand-up bar for parties or as bar seating for weeknight family dinners. The broad, connecting counter in between can be used by two or more people at the same time for food preparation. It also doubles as a buffet counter at serving time. A variety of built-in storage cabinets are included in the stone base, which was built using a sturdy, noncorrosive, but easy-to-assemble anodized aluminum frame.

A separate set of base and wall cabinets are located just steps away against the garage wall. These modular polymer cabinets were chosen for their extensive storage capacity. A sink and under-counter refrigerator make this the preferred food preparation and cleanup area for larger gatherings, allowing the homeowners to reserve the I-counter for food service.

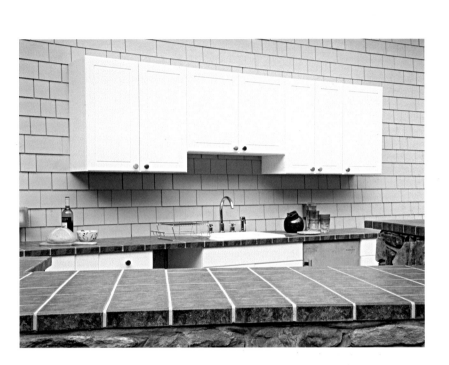

above • The wall cabinets are used for storing paper goods, nonbreakable dinnerware, and plenty of plastic cups for use around the pool.

above • This outdoor kitchen uses a combination of cabinet styles: a stone island built on a modular frame and ready-made modular cabinets made from marine-grade polymer. Both are finished with a blue-tile top.

facing page • Equipped with many conveniences, the island features a tilt-out trash can, lots of stainless-steel drawers, and even a long compartment in the end counter for storing the umbrella when not in use (above).

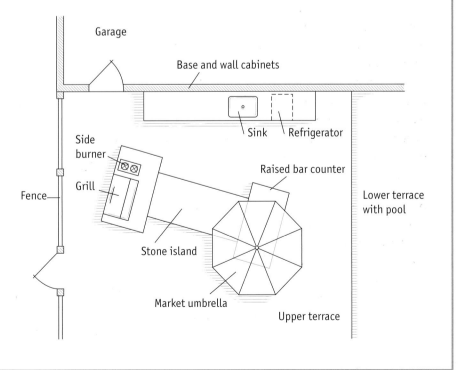

Organizing Ideas

A well-organized outdoor kitchen lets you spend time having fun or focusing on your guests rather than looking for the right tool or condiment. Some organizing tools, such as plastic bins, not only keep your supplies in order but also keep them clean and dry, a real issue in most outdoor kitchens. Others—such as boxes, baskets, and drawer organizers—make it easier to find what you're looking for, to set the table, or to clean up after a meal.

1. An office organizer doubles as a kitchen caddy for napkins and utensils **2.** Dish racks aren't just for drying. This one displays a collection of colorful melamine plates on an open shelf. **3.** Tabletop containers and canisters keep utensils where you need them. Just stash the container in a cabinet when the kitchen is not in use. **4.** This small wire basket makes it easy to carry condiments to the table. **5.** Clear plastic storage bins keep supplies clean, dry, and easy to find.

Sinks

Sinks are a welcome addition to any outdoor kitchen and essential for those located at any distance from the house. Although small bar sinks are common, bigger and deeper is almost always better. With a large sink, you can rinse serving platters, fill up stockpots with water, and wash a basketful of garden beans or tomatoes. Of the different styles available are these:

- Drop-in sinks, which fit into a hole cut into the counter, are the easiest to install.
- Undermount sinks are easier to clean than drop-in sinks, but more difficult to install and require a perfect, polished-edge cutout.
- Farmhouse sinks are freestanding basins that are mounted flush with the cabinet front, making them easier to reach than other sinks.
- Integrated sinks feature seamless construction that makes them an integrated part of the counter.
- Vessel sinks are small, decorative bowls that sit on top of the counter.
- Bar centers consisting of bar sinks, coolers, and condiment bins are preassembled units that drop into a counter like a farm-house sink.

Stainless steel is, by far, the most popular material for outdoor sinks because it weathers well, is available in a wide range of styles and price ranges, and is easy to install. Porcelain enamel looks like ceramic but will better withstand weather conditions. Stone basins are extremely durable, and copper will develop a beautiful patina as it ages. Like sinks, most outdoor faucets are made from stainless steel. Those with solid brass insides and ceramic disk valves will last the longest.

Most outdoor sinks, unless they are intended for dishwashing, can get by with cold water only. This can be supplied by a water line from the house or a garden hose. If hot water is desired, it can be run from the house or cold water can be heated by a small, undersink water heater.

In most cases, the sink's drain line will be tied into the home's main drainage system or a separate dry well. An alternative to this approach is to install a gray-water tank: Water from this tank can be used for watering the landscape—though only biodegradable soaps that are not toxic to plants should be used in the sink. For sinks that get minimal use, it's possible to simply collect the water beneath the sink in 5-gallon or 10-gallon buckets and then dispose of it.

above • This stainless-steel door provides access to sink plumbing—necessary for all sinks. The cavity and door are large enough to double as a storage cabinet for cleaning supplies as well.

left • This stainless-steel undermount sink is located right next to the back door. In addition to serving the outdoor kitchen, it's perfect for washing up after yard work before heading back indoors. The soap dispenser is considered a must-have.

below • Since the indoor kitchen is located just on the other side of the wall, a bar sink was sufficient in this outdoor room. It's used mostly for mixing drinks, rinsing utensils, and moistening a cloth to wipe down the counter.

Sink Materials

Stainless steel rules in outdoor kitchens thanks to its durability and availability in a variety of shapes, sizes, and price ranges. But other sink styles are gaining in popularity as outdoor kitchens become more elaborate. Sinks that can scratch, stain, or chip are best used beneath the shelter or roof, if at all, whereas more durable sinks are better choices for open settings. To improve the life span of a sink, cover it in winter to keep out water, which could collect and freeze, and to keep out debris that might stain finishes or clog drains. All sinks should have a shut-off valve that allows them to be drained before freezing temperatures set in.

SOLID-SURFACE SINK

STAINLESS STEEL
$–$$$

- Easy to clean
- Durable and noncorrosive
- Brushed finished wears best outdoors

POLISHED STONE
$$$

- Available in granite and soapstone
- Durable and noncorrosive
- Must be sealed periodically
- Soapstone can chip

SOLID SURFACE
$$

- Can be fabricated to create a seamless sink and counter
- Wide range of colors, shapes, sizes, and styles
- Reasonably scratch and dent resistant
- Not heat resistant next to grill
- Color runs through core, so scratches can be sanded out

PORCELAIN ENAMEL
$$

- Wide range of colors, sizes, and styles
- Can be burned by hot pots and pans
- Can scratch and stain
- Best used in covered area

CONCRETE
$$–$$$

- Durable
- Can be molded to create a seamless sink and counter
- Color can be custom mixed
- Must be sealed to prevent staining, keep out dirt, and prevent cracking

COPPER
$$

- Rugged good looks
- Develops beautiful patina
- Can dent, tarnish, and stain

STAINLESS-STEEL SINK

POLISHED GRANITE VESSEL SINK

Sinks and Faucets

In addition to the various mounting styles and materials, sinks come in a wide range of shapes and sizes. Faucets are equally diverse. Choose from knobs or levers, single-handled or double-handled, with long necks or short necks, fixed positions or adjustable, and with or without sprayers and soap dispensers. Each type comes in a range of materials and finishes.

1. Old plumbing parts were used to create this one-of-a-kind faucet that spills into a large copper basin. 2. The long neck on this faucet is positioned high so large pots and platters can be placed in the sink with ease. 3. With a base that echoes the shape of the bowl, this kitchen sink is a focal point of the kitchen. 4. Oversize basins are ideal for outdoor sinks. In addition to usual kitchen duties, they can be used for watering pots of plants or washing a small dog.

Cold Storage

Topping the list of the most useful outdoor cold-storage appliances is the under-counter refrigerator. Though these units are small—usually just 15 in. or 24 in. wide—they save many trips into the house for cold drinks and frequently used condiments. When preparing and cooking meals, they are also perfect for short-term storage to keep food out of the heat. Compare models for shelf configuration: Some may have door racks or separate wine shelves in addition to standard shelving. A few have built-in ice makers, though a freezer is rare.

Under-counter wine coolers come in a range of sizes, often with two temperature zones—one for white wines and another for red (because outdoor summer temperatures are rarely suitable for storing red wines). Beer dispensers, which generally hold half or quarter kegs, are especially convenient for parties. Ice makers are another convenience item well suited for outdoor use on a hot day or when entertaining.

Cold-storage outdoor appliances are built from stainless steel—though some feature glass-front doors. Although they are most commonly built into cabinetry, many are designed for freestanding use as well. All run on standard household current, but should be UL-rated for outdoor use and plugged in only to a GFCI outlet. If the units aren't front venting, a vent will need to be built into the cabinetry.

Even with a refrigerator or wine cooler, you'll find that portable coolers—an insulated chest or open bucket even—still have their place outdoors. Sinks not being used for food preparation can also double as a cooler for short-term beverage service.

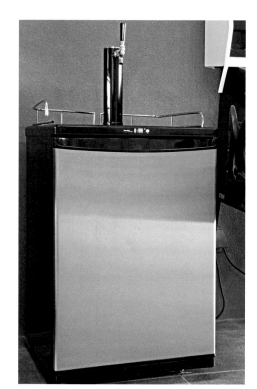

right • This full-size beer dispenser holds a half, quarter, or mini keg. It features an attractive draft tower, drip tray, and adjustable thermostat. Small casters make it portable, as long as it can be plugged into an electrical outlet.

right • A standard 24-in.-wide, UL-rated outdoor refrigerator slides right under the counter for convenience. It features a combination of flat shelving and door racks for maximum storage capacity.

above • At only 15 in. wide, this refrigerator fits into tight spaces. The sleek design features a brushed stainless-steel door with a contrasting polished stainless-steel handle. The extra height compensates for the loss in width.

left • For wine enthusiasts who entertain often or those who host large parties, a wine cooler is a practical way to store both white and red wine outdoors, where temperatures often exceed those normally suitable for proper bottle storage.

Portable Beverage Coolers

No outdoor kitchen—not even those with under-counter refrigerators—should be without at least one portable beverage cooler. Outdoor refrigerators are small, so portable coolers come in handy when hosting a party or when the fridge is filled with food. Choose from commercially available coolers or place interesting metal containers into temporary service for chilling your favorite beverages. If possible, keep coolers in the shade so the ice won't melt too fast.

1. Antique containers of all kinds can be filled with ice and cold drinks. 2. Raised up on legs, this barrel-style beverage cooler puts drinks within easy reach. 3. Large galvanized buckets are great for chilling bottled and canned beverages. Be sure to set them in a place where they can sweat. 4. With food preparation finished, this sink fills in as a cooler at serving time. 5. This teak cooler looks good enough to leave out full time and doubles as a bench or small side table when not chilling beverages.

Cabinets

The role of outdoor cabinets, either portable or built-in, is threefold—to structurally link and support outdoor appliances, to serve as a base for counter work surfaces, and to provide storage. Portable cabinets are generally economical alternatives to built-in cabinetry and can be just as beautiful and functional. Think grilling carts, bar carts, potting benches, and commercial-kitchen work tables.

Permanent cabinets run the gamut from off-the-shelf to ready-to-assemble to totally custom. And with these options come a range of prices for both the cabinets themselves and installation. Consider the following choices in permanent cabinets:

- Ready-made grilling islands are built on steel frames and are available with exterior finishes, countertops, appliances, and doors already installed.

- Ready-made modular cabinets are made of stainless steel or marine-grade polymer. Select the modules you need, connect them with filler panels, and add a countertop.

- Modular framing systems, made from steel or anodized aluminum, screw together to create cabinet modules. Concrete backer board is attached to the frame, which then supports your choice of exterior finish.

- Custom wood frames are built entirely on site, based on your own plans. Like modular framing systems, they are then surrounded by concrete backer board and finished with exterior materials.

- Custom masonry frames are built from concrete block and finished with exterior materials.

Cabinet exteriors or veneers must be made of durable, exterior-grade materials. Except for warm, dry, well-sheltered locations, most interior-grade finishes are not suitable for outdoor use. Today's exterior grade choices are attractive, durable, and designed to blend in well with a home's architecture or surrounding landscape. In addition to stainless steel and polymer, these include rot-resistant woods such as mahogany, teak, ipe, cedar, and redwood; traditional house siding and cedar shingles; natural or engineered (synthetic) stone; and brick, tile, and stucco.

Storage Bench

This built-in mahogany bench doubles as a cabinet. Just lift up the seat and there's plenty of storage space beneath. It is perfectly sized to contain seat cushions, furniture or grill covers, a portable cooler, or balls for backyard games. Used as a filler cabinet along one end of a small deck, it proves that small or awkward spaces can be put to good use.

above • This grilling island doubles as a wall along one side of a small patio, just steps away from the dining area. Here, it takes up minimal space and helps screen neighboring backyards. A masonry block frame was finished in stone and topped with granite for a clean, crisp look. There's ample counter space on either side of the charcoal grill for food prep and serving; the large drawer stores cleaning supplies.

Built-In Cabinetry

Although there's a range of cabinetry types available, most retailers stock only a few types; and depending on the type of professional you're working with, he or she might not know all the fine details of the many kinds. For example, most designers, builders, or barbecue specialty companies offer only one or two cabinet types. Homebuilders are more accustomed to working with custom wood framing, and landscape architects may be more familiar with custom masonry construction or modular framing systems. And home centers and specialty grilling stores may offer only ready-made grilling islands or modular cabinets. So it's helpful to know the pros and cons of each system and to talk with several companies before making a final decision.

READY-MADE GRILLING ISLANDS
$

- Installed quickly and easily
- Lighter weight materials (for easy moving)
- Limited to manufacturer's designs

READY-MADE MODULAR CABINETS
$$

- Flexible design
- Ample storage
- Traditional indoor kitchen styles

MODULAR FRAMING SYSTEMS
$$–$$$

- Flexible design
- Custom finish and counter
- Ample storage
- Nonflammable

CUSTOM WOOD FRAMES
$$–$$$

- Completely custom
- Flexible design
- Ample storage
- Frame is flammable

CUSTOM MASONRY FRAMES
$$–$$$

- Extremely durable
- Classic outdoor kitchen look
- More difficult to design storage
- Nonflammable

READY-MADE MODULAR CABINET

CUSTOM MASONRY CABINET

MODULAR FRAME WITH STUCCO FINISH

Exterior Cabinet Finishes

The choice of an exterior cabinet finish is an aesthetic and budgetary decision. It should be based on your personal style preferences, the materials that best complement your home's architecture or blend into your local landscape, and the funds that you have allocated for cabinetry construction.

NATURAL STONE
$$–$$$

- Extremely durable
- Natural looking; blends with landscape
- Nonflammable

ENGINEERED STONE
$$

- Looks like stone; blends with landscape
- Nonflammable

BRICK
$

- Traditional look, so blends well with that style of architecture
- Durable
- Nonflammable

PORCELAIN TILE
$

- Variety of colors, sizes, styles available
- Blends in with architecture
- Durable and nonflammable
- Choose material suited for local climate

STUCCO
$

- Variety of colors available
- Clean, simple finish

POLYMER
$

- Impervious
- Available in range of colors

STAINLESS STEEL
$$$

- Extremely durable
- Sleek, contemporary look
- Nonflammable

ROT-RESISTANT WOOD
$–$$

- Cedar, redwood, mahogany, teak, and ipe
- Can use siding to match house
- Flammable

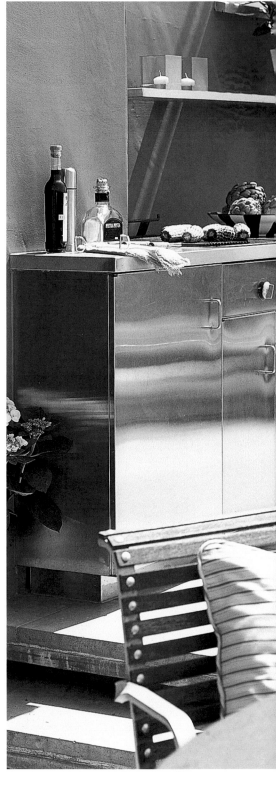

STAINLESS-STEEL FINISH

CEDAR-SHINGLE VENEER

STACKED-STONE EXTERIOR

Laying Out the Components

It helps to think in terms of modules when configuring any outdoor kitchen, even one without permanent cabinetry. This makes it easy to figure out which components you need, roughly how much space each should occupy, and how they should relate to each other.

When laying out the components, keep in mind that sinks, grills, and side burners occupy counter space, while under-counter refrigerators, storage cabinets, warming ovens, and drawers do not. Though it's common to place grills and side burners side by side, it's important to leave some counter space on at least one side of the grill and preferably both sides of the sink. In other words, avoid placing a grill and sink side by side if at all possible. A longer run of counter space is often more versatile than two or three very short runs, but consider where you need the counter space the most and design accordingly. Sometimes you'll need connecting segments—frequently referred to as filler panels—to tie everything together or fill awkward gaps. Angled corner cabinets are useful for adapting your layout to a specific space or desired configuration.

When laying out the components, don't forget to think in terms of hot, cold, wet, and dry zones as well as how these different areas relate to each other functionally. Sinks and refrigerators, for instance, may be important for both food preparation and beverage service, so they should be placed in close proximity of one another, if not right next to each other. Also, remember that the grill should be positioned downwind and away from high-traffic areas. If guests will be using certain components, such as a drop-in cooler or refrigerator, positioning them near dining or entertaining areas to help keep kitchen traffic to a minimum.

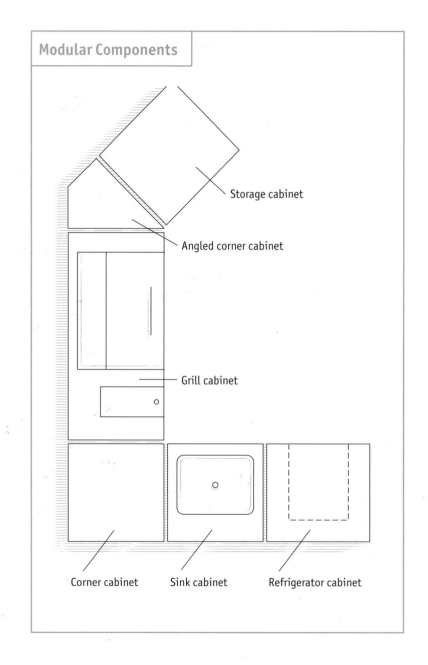

Modular Components

Storage cabinet

Angled corner cabinet

Grill cabinet

Corner cabinet   Sink cabinet   Refrigerator cabinet

facing page • This cabinet is totally modular. It includes a grilling cabinet, a single-drawer/double-door cabinet, and two single-drawer/single-door cabinets. The matching glass doors add an interesting visual element to the sleek cabinetry design.

Built-In Cabinets

Cabinets can be configured in any number of ways. The straight run, galley, L-shaped, U-shaped, and G-shaped layouts are most common. They can be placed against a wall, along the edge of a patio, or as a freestanding island. They may or may not include overhead cabinets, and the materials they are finished with can be used in surprisingly creative ways.

1. The angled grilling cabinet was built into a synthetic boulder to help it blend into the landscape. **2.** This kitchen cabinet was finished with a veneer of poles to match the hut. **3.** Mahogany cabinets built on an anodized aluminum frame enclose a small deck to create the feeling of an outdoor room. **4.** Barn-style sliding doors that match the kitchen cabinets can be closed to hide the clutter at dinnertime or to protect the kitchen when not in use.

Cabinet Doors and Hardware

Ready-made grilling islands and modular cabinets come with their own doors and drawers. For any other type of cabinet, you'll need to purchase or build doors. Most manufacturers of drop-in grills offer stainless-steel or powder-coated-steel doors. Custom doors can also be built from teak, cedar, mahogany, or other rot-resistant wood. Be sure to use fasteners that won't rust as well.

1. Stainless-steel doors match the grill, sink, and side burner to create a unified look in this outdoor kitchen. 2. Brushed steel panels in the cabinet doors were custom designed to match the grill. 3. These heavy, redwood-plank doors are accented by hand-forged wrought-iron hardware. 4. This wood-panel door was inset in the masonry cavity to enhance the cabinet's clean lines.

Built-In Conveniences

When designing outdoor cabinets, don't forget about those little things you may need in your kitchen such as paper towels, trash bins, towels, and bottle openers. Manufacturers have introduced many convenience-oriented built-ins that will fit most outdoor cabinets; more options will likely be introduced in the coming years. Just remember that you'll need to provide a list of all drop-in units and their installation dimensions to your cabinet builder.

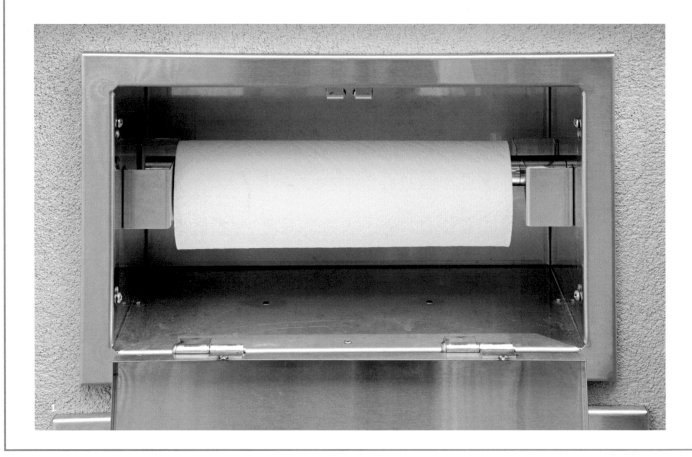

1. This recessed paper-towel holder keeps the towels dry, handy, and off the counter. **2.** A towel bar and bottle opener (with its own catch bin) are invaluable at parties and appreciated any time. **3.** Just tilt the door and toss in your trash. This is a great way to keep the trash bin out of sight, yet convenient. **4.** Propane tanks, especially when full, can be clumsy to handle. This pullout drawer is a back-saver.

Counters

Counters really pull an outdoor kitchen together, both visually and functionally. They are the surface we see and use most often, and the surface that takes the most abuse. Not only must they withstand hot platters, sharp knives, spilled drinks, and occasional dropped dishes but they must also weather sun, rain, snow, ice, and falling tree limbs. So, first and foremost, counters must be durable. That means watertight; fade and stain resistant; scratch and chip resistant; and heat and frost tolerant.

If your budget permits splurging on just one item, you'll get the most for your money by investing in a quality counter. For starters, counters take the most abuse, so it pays to invest in durable materials. But they're also the element most often viewed close up, so you can make a good impression with quality materials. Most outdoor counters have a relatively small footprint, so it's often possible to upgrade the materials without breaking the budget. For these reasons—extreme durability and sheer beauty—polished stone counters are among the most popular choices in outdoor counters.

Beyond polished stones such as granite and soapstone, other good choices for outdoor counters include unpolished stone slab, flagstone, stone tile, porcelain tile, stainless steel, and concrete (which can be stained just about any color and polished to a beautiful finish). Unpolished stone and concrete should be sealed to prevent staining and deterioration.

Backsplashes and special counter edges—such as bull-nose or cantilevered edges—can also enhance your outdoor kitchen. Although backsplashes are less common in outdoor kitchens than in indoor kitchens, they are still practical for protecting adjacent walls from spills and splashes. Even more common, backsplashes are used to screen the backside of a grill from view, which has the added benefit of providing a windbreak.

Choosing the Right Tile

The most durable tiles for outdoor use are polished stone and unglazed porcelain. Polished stone tiles made from granite, soapstone, or quartz offer the same beauty and durability as stone slab except that they require grouting and cost less because they are made from smaller pieces of stone. Among ceramic tiles, porcelain is the most durable. It is harder than stone and impervious to water. which means that it can endure freeze–thaw cycles without cracking. It is also a through-body tile, so if it is scratched or chipped, the tile remains the same color throughout. In climates where freezing temperatures are not a concern, nonporcelain or glazed tiles are an option for backsplashes but not for counter surfaces, because they can be easily damaged in outdoor settings.

above · The granite surface on this extension table is the same used for the kitchen counter. It has a bull-nose edge and rests on a wrought-iron post. Not wanting to waste space, the owners tucked a refrigerator in the cabinet at the end of the table.

right · This decorative stone and tile backsplash adds an attractive visual element to the outdoor kitchen. It's functional as well—screening the back of the grill from view (there's a path on the back side) and cutting down on drafts.

facing page · The narrow stand-up bar features a slab granite surface, and the kitchen counter was set with matching granite tiles. Wide slabs of stone are considerably more expensive than smaller tiles, so this was a cost-effective way to use the material.

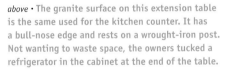

Counter Materials

Countertops are available in both natural and synthetic materials, making it easy to select a surface that suits your home's style and that stands up to local climate conditions. Ceramic tile, laminates, and woods are generally not good choices for outdoor settings because they may fade, stain, crack, or warp.

SEALED BLUESTONE SLAB COUNTER

POLISHED STONE
$$$
- Choose from granite, marble, soapstone, and quartz
- Extremely durable finish
- Resists scratching, staining, and fading
- Smooth, handsome surface

ENGINEERED STONE
$$–$$$
- Mostly stone, with less than 10 percent synthetic composite
- Quartz products are stronger than stone
- Resists scratching, staining, and fading
- Wide range of colors

PORCELAIN TILE
$
- Durable
- Wide range of colors and textures
- Multiple shapes, sizes, and trim pieces can be mixed and matched

FLAGSTONE
$$
- Durable
- Natural looking
- Variety in stone color, shape, size, and texture
- Should be sealed to prevent stains

POLISHED GRANITE COUNTER

CONCRETE
$$–$$$
- Extremely durable
- Rugged good looks; can add color and texture to vary appearance
- Must be sealed to prevent staining, to keep out dirt, and to prevent cracking from freeze–thaw cycle

STAINLESS STEEL
$$$
- Durable, rust resistant and easy to clean
- Sleek, professional styling
- Can get very hot when exposed to sun

SOLID SURFACE
$$
- Not heat resistant next to grill; use in other locations
- Can be fabricated to create a seamless sink and counter
- Wide range of colors
- Can scratch or dent
- Color runs through core, so scratches can be sanded out

SEALED FLAGSTONE COUNTER

Counters

When designing counters, think beyond the rectangle. Curved counters can add visual interest and make it easier for guests to visit with each other and the chef. Counters set at different heights look great and can serve different purposes in the outdoor kitchen. Also, don't just think in terms of a single counter material. Try mixing and matching materials for eye-catching results.

1. This curved bump-up counter provides a comfortable seating area that faces the chef. 2. Smooth Devonshire marble was used for both the counter and backsplash and was capped off with a row of contrasting Bitterroot stone for accent. 3. This bump-up counter runs the length of the kitchen cabinets. It serves as a bar and helps screen the food preparation surfaces from general view. 4. Different colors and sizes of tumbled travertine tile were mixed and matched to create a tile band on the backsplash.

A Rustic Retreat

These weathered, board-and-batten buildings bring to mind old farmhouse compounds from the past. Although this one was recently constructed, it suits the farmland-turned-vineyard site in California's Napa Valley. It features three buildings—the main house, a smaller guesthouse, and the garage—connected by breezeways and outdoor living spaces.

Here, everything is in keeping with the site. Boulders cleared from the land when preparing soil for planting were used to build the surrounds for the wood-burning oven. The large, beamed pergola is in perfect scale with the house. Beneath it, an oversize, wide-plank picnic table hosts casual outdoor gatherings with extended family and friends. Even the barn-style light fixtures over the outdoor kitchen counter look as if they'd been hanging there for ages.

The kitchen cabinets, built along one wall of the guest wing, blend right in. The rugged, redwood doors are simply framed and subtly accented with black, hand-wrought hardware you'd expect to find around a farm. The indoor kitchen, located in the main house near the arbor, features large glass doors that are left open to the patio on warm days. Because of the kitchen's close proximity, the outdoor cabinets are used to store firewood rather than kitchen supplies. The wood is used in the pizza oven, in a fire pit located just beyond the patio, and in the outdoor fireplace located through the breezeway in the courtyard garden. As friends gather on the weekend or for special occasions, large stoneware containers filled with fresh vegetables, fruits, and flowers are spread out buffet-style along the long, stone counter.

top • Firewood for the pizza oven, fire pit, and fireplace are stored beneath the kitchen counters. The drawers were built on heavy-duty rollers to make loading and unloading a breeze.

right • The wedge-shaped patio spans the space between the kitchen and guesthouse. Pizzas are cooked in the wood-burning oven to feed hungry family members, who gather around the picnic tables beneath the pergola.

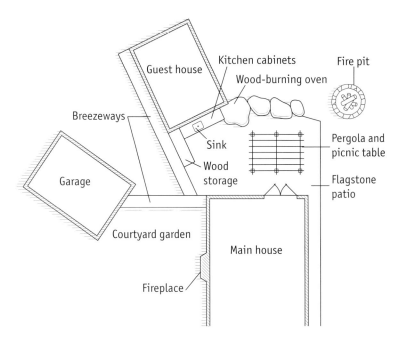

Garage

Breezeways

Guest house

Kitchen cabinets

Wood-burning oven

Fire pit

Sink

Wood storage

Pergola and picnic table

Flagstone patio

Courtyard garden

Main house

Fireplace

above • This outdoor lighting is so subtle that you almost overlook it. Two barn-style lamps provide most of the light, while a single strip light mounted beneath the window seal provides additional illumination for the sink.

left • These redwood cabinets were designed with simple lines to complement the board-and-batten farmhouse architecture. Forged-iron hardware suits the rugged cabinetry.

EATING

When designing an outdoor dining area, think in terms of comfort and ambience. Stylish furniture, colorful table settings, soft lighting, and even the right music all help to create the perfect setting for an al fresco meal.

AREAS

Designing a Space for Dining

The first step in designing a dining area is selecting a suitable location. It must be large enough to accommodate the right furniture—whether that's a bistro table for 2, a round dining set for 4, a rectangular extension table with seating for 12, or multiple tables for a crowd. A good rule of thumb is to leave a minimum of 3 ft. on each side of the table for moving the chairs about or walking behind a seated guest and at least 5 ft. between a table and any steps for safety reasons. This will create a cozy, yet comfortable dining area. For a more spacious feeling, simply give the table more breathing room. Other space considerations include whether you need a buffet table for serving food or a bar for serving drinks. You might also consider creating bar seating that is built into the kitchen counter. A bar counter is a fun place to hang out in any outdoor kitchen and offers a practical solution for dining where space is limited.

Once you've identified potential locations, observe the sun and shade patterns at different times of the day and consider how they change at different times of the year. Based on your local climate conditions, do you need a place in the sun, a spot in the shade, or both? If you need both, multiple dining areas are a great solution if space isn't an issue. Or if your site is sunny, opt for a market umbrella or retractable awning that can be used to create shade only when needed. Arbors covered in deciduous vines let the sun shine through in early spring and fall, but provide dense shade in summer once established. Structures with solid roofs, such as porches or pavilions, create year-round protection from both sun and rain.

And, finally, think about the atmosphere you are creating—select comfortable, stylish furniture; provide privacy or weather protection with screening or roofs; and enhance the space with light, sound, or perhaps even an outdoor hearth.

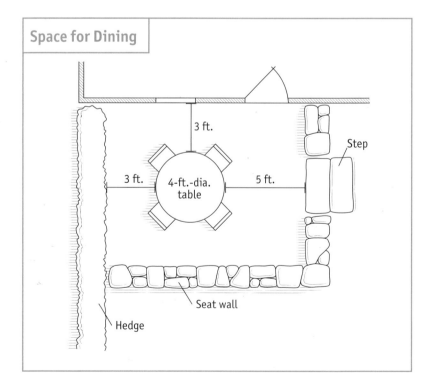

Space for Dining

3 ft.

Step

3 ft.   4-ft.-dia. table   5 ft.

Seat wall

Hedge

facing page • Designed for entertaining, this backyard pavilion features strong lines and striking architectural materials such as metal beams and a unique stainless-steel fireplace screen that is raised and lowered with a pulley system.

right • Bistro tables, like this one with a mosaic-tile top, are ideal for romantic dinners. They are also perfect for one person—whether it's for a leisurely breakfast, quick lunch, or working from home on the laptop.

below • This patio features two dining areas. The main area has a round table with seating for four and is used primarily for family dinners. The second, at the far end of the patio, features a rectangular table with seating for eight that is used for entertaining.

Craftsman-Style Pergola Complements House Renovation

When these homeowners purchased a recently renovated Craftsman-style house, the front yard had been redesigned, but the backyard was waiting its turn for a makeover. The owners contacted the landscape architect who had designed the front so the property would have a consistent look throughout.

Because the couple has young children and enjoy entertaining, the backyard needed a combination of kids' play space and adult entertaining space. So the youngsters got a game lawn and a small paved pad next to the shed for riding tricycles and shooting hoops. And for the adults, a spacious patio with a Craftsman-style, grapevine-covered arbor was built.

Using mostly reddish toned flagstone, bricks, and ceramic tiles, the patio was laid in what is commonly referred to as a crazy paving style. Smooth, rounded river cobbles were added here and there for accent. The overall effect is much like that of a richly colored tapestry rug: lots of texture and plenty to look at. Overhead, a pergola with Craftsman-style hardware and lighting fixtures (to complement the home) was constructed, and grapevines are now being trained up each post. Beneath the pergola sits a teak dining table with seating for eight—just the right size for dinner parties or kids' birthday parties.

A modest deck just beyond the backdoor was also turned into functional dining space by building seats into the railing and adding a small table with two chairs. Two can dine here comfortably; four can make it work in a pinch. It's an especially nice place for the kids to work on crafts projects or to eat with their friends while the grownups dine at the big table nearby.

right • A second, much smaller dining area can be found on the small deck beyond the backdoor. There's just enough room for a table and two chairs, but bench seating around the edge of the deck makes it possible to seat four.

left • Sturdy 6×6 posts support 4×4 beams and several runs of heavy-gauge marine-grade cable. Over time, the fruiting vines will cover the pergola to create a densely shaded dining and entertaining area.

below • The pergola features a Craftsman-style wall sconce and custom-designed ironwork that tie in with the architecture of the house. There are four sconces in all, which provide general patio illumination. Candles placed on the table add atmosphere and extra light for eating.

left • The floor of this outdoor room is covered in crazy paving— mix-and-match materials combined in random patterns for interest underfoot. This particular mixture includes flagstone, brick, tiles, and river cobbles, all carefully color coordinated.

Bar Seating

Outdoor kitchens are a lot like indoor kitchens in that everyone congregates around the cook. Spaces that are designed with this in mind make some of the most successful outdoor gathering spaces. A well-designed outdoor kitchen can give guests a comfortable place to visit with the chef while keeping them out of the work area. And one of the easiest ways to do this is to build bar seating that faces the cooking area—though at least several feet away from the heat and smoke of the grill. Once the food has been cooked, this same space can double as a dining area.

Although most backyard bars can't seat as many people as a large table, they are perfect for casual weeknight dinners, afternoon snacks for the kids, and overflow seating during a party. Without stools, these counters make perfect stand-up bars for cocktail buffets or a convenient spot for serving food buffet-style (as long as it's not too high).

Most kitchen counters are approximately 36 in. high. A counter can be extended beyond the cabinet base at that same height to accommodate seating on medium-height stools. This is also the best height for serving food buffet style. Traditional bar seating with a bump-up counter is higher—approximately 42 in.—and accommodates tall stools or bar chairs. It is also a convenient height for serving finger foods and drinks. Whether low or high, the counter overhang should be 8 in. to 12 in. deep to prevent knees from knocking the cabinet when seated. Another option is to create a 5-ft. or 6-ft. table extension at roughly the same height as the counter; it rests on the counter or a base cabinet at one end and a pedestal at the other end. Allow 2½ ft. to 3 ft. per seat, depending on the width of the stool or chair and whether or not it swivels.

above • This seating area was created by extending the grilling island 4 ft. beyond the last appliance (an under-counter refrigerator) and food-preparation area. The end of the counter is cut in a circle, which allows guests to face each other as well as the chef.

left • This bar counter is designed for socializing while dinner is being grilled and can serve as extra dinner seating. The raised counter also helps screen the food-preparation area from view so the outdoor room retains its clean, crisp look even when there are dirty dishes on the counter.

Covered Dining Areas

Dining beneath the sun or moon is a delightful experience, but in many climates, an overhead structure is essential for protection from frequent rain showers or blistering sun. In urban and suburban settings, where neighbors are located nearby, such a structure can help create a more private experience. Even if it's not needed for privacy or shelter, a roof of some sort helps create a cozy atmosphere and may serve as a support for hanging lights and fans or be incorporated into the support system for the outdoor kitchen area.

Covered dining areas can be permanent or temporary and with either an open or solid roof. Market umbrellas and retractable awnings (which can be opened or closed as needed) and party tents (which can be erected for festive occasions or left up for the entire season) are both affordable and flexible. Permanent structures such as arbors and pergolas won't keep out the rain, but they help define a space and create an inviting and shady setting. Covered with wisteria, roses, or other fragrant vines, they can produce a romantic atmosphere. A sailcloth roof is another alternative for shade. It comes in standard and custom shapes and sizes and can be attached to existing structures or poles specifically designed for its use.

If a solid-roof overhead is more desirable—whether from an aesthetic standpoint, for rain protection, or to permit complete enclosure with screened walls—consider creating a dining area beneath the cover of a porch, portico, or pool house or building a gazebo or pavilion. Garden structures such as arbors, pergolas, pavilions, and gazebos provide a focal point in the landscape and can be placed either on a patio for convenience or farther out in the landscape to create a unique destination for outdoor dining. The outdoor kitchen can be built adjacent to or even beneath this structure for convenience and protection.

above • This broad umbrella rests on a freestanding base that can be moved as the sun shifts in the sky. It can also be dropped or moved aside if not needed.

DETAILS THAT WORK

Low-Maintenance Pergola

Instead of using wood columns and beams to build this pergola, the designer used fabricated, powder-coated steel beams and cast-concrete columns with steel posts (for internal structural support). These alternative materials not only keep the pergola looking fresh and new but greatly reduce ongoing maintenance because they won't rot and will rarely, if ever, need to be painted.

facing page • Curtain rods and sheer white curtains were added to this wooden pergola to create a light, airy dining room. A tiered candlelight chandelier was hung from the overhead beams to help create a romantic atmosphere after dark.

Shade Structures

Nothing beats the comfort and charm of an old shade tree, but if your property isn't blessed with one, shade can be created with manufactured structures while the trees you plant mature for future generations. Some of these structures are considered partof the house, and others are distinctly part of the garden. Some keep out the rain as well as the sun. And some can be adjusted according to the weather, time of day, or season.

PERGOLA OR ARBOR
$$

- Arbors are attached to the house and can shade interior rooms as well
- Pergolas are freestanding elements in the landscape
- Offer shade but not protection from rain
- Can be covered with fragrant vines
- Usually permanent structures that require minimal maintenance

PAVILION OR GAZEBO
$$–$$$

- Offer both shade and protection from rain
- Permanent structures that require maintenance
- Usually require a poured foundation
- Can be designed to reflect architecture of home

PORTICO OR PORCH
$$$

- Offer both shade and protection from rain
- Permanent structures that are part of the house
- May require a permit to build
- Can often be screened

AWNING
$$

- Attached to the house
- Offers shade and light rain protection
- May be retractable
- Many color choices

MARKET UMBRELLA
$

- Portable—use with table or freestanding
- Offers shade but only minimal rain protection
- Many color choices
- Can be opened or closed as needed

SAIL CLOTH
$$

- Offers shade only
- Many color, shape, and size choices
- A stylish option
- Can be custom designed

PERGOLA

SAILCLOTH

AWNING

PORTICO

An Attached Dining Arbor

The only thing left standing in this yard after fire swept through the Oakland Hills in 1991 was a dilapidated pool house located at the rear of the property. The main house, a Craftsman-styled stucco home, was rebuilt from the ground up. The pool house was renovated to complement the home's architecture and now doubles as a portrait photography studio and guesthouse. The landscape was completely redesigned; instead of the pool, a spa was placed on the guesthouse deck. Curving stone walls that anchor a mixed garden border connect the guesthouse with the back-yard patio located just beyond the home's back door.

The redesign was a collaborative process among an architect, a landscape architect, and the homeowners. It was during the planning process that the architect noticed how the two-story facade towered over the relatively small backyard. That's when the idea for a built-in dining arbor was born. It was conceived to give the rear of the house greater visual and structural interest, to better tie the house to the landscape, and to create an intimate area for outdoor living. Tucked into the corner of the patio and surrounded by a Japanese maple and ornamental grasses, it has become a private alcove that overlooks the more public areas of yard. Located just steps from the back door, it is convenient to the kitchen. A gas grill resides nearby on the flagstone patio, which is used for entertaining and family activities.

left • Benches built along two sides of the arbor echo the Craftsman-style detailing found inside as well as on the front of the house. The paint matches the home's trim color, making it feel as if the arbor were part of the original architecture (even though it was an added feature).

above • In addition to providing shade and a ceiling overhead, the arbor provides a place to mount outdoor lighting. These two Craftsman-style fixtures provide ample illumination for the dining area without being distracting or overpowering.

above • The arbor creates a ceiling overhead, while the posts define the corners of this outdoor dining room. Vines are encouraged to wend their way up the posts and across the beams for added privacy and shade.

right • The dining arbor is tucked away in the corner of the patio where it forms a cozy alcove. The patio extends out into the yard and offers a casual seating area in the sun as well as a place to entertain.

Dining Tables and Chairs

Dining tables and chairs come in a range of shapes, sizes, styles, and materials to suit just about any need. Bistro sets, which offer cozy seating for 2, are small enough to fit even the smallest patios and garden rooms. Dining sets, which seat from 4 to 12, come in round, oval, square, and rectangular shapes and are often available with extension leaves for varying the table size. Bar-height sets, which are 39-in. to 42-in. high (rather than the standard 28-in. to 30-in. height of most dining sets), are designed to seat 2 or 4. When choosing tables, it's important to know how many people you will normally seat and what style of chair you prefer. Wide armchairs or swiveling chairs can easily occupy 25 percent more space than a standard side chair. Even so, the following sizes offer a good starting point when shopping for a table or designating space for a table on your porch, patio, or deck.

- 30-in.- to 36-in.-long tables seat 2.
- 38-in.- to 48-in.-long tables seat 4.
- 54-in.- to 60-in.-long tables seat 4 to 6.
- 72-in.- to 80-in.-long tables seat 6 to 10 (or more with extension leaves)

Table and chair materials run the gamut from exotic tropical hardwoods to all-weather wicker to powder-coated metals (see "Designing an Outdoor Room," starting on p. 159). Choose furniture based on style, weight, and durability—avoiding anything that will rust, splinter, or easily rot. If your style of entertaining involves long evenings around the dinner table or if you don't have another comfortable seating area to migrate to when the meal is over, consider cushioned dining chairs for extended comfort. Make sure cushions are designed for outdoor use and covered in water-resistant fabrics that won't fade or mildew. Choose from classic, contemporary, tropical, or rustic design styles to complement your home and outdoor kitchen.

Lighter weight pieces are the easiest to move, especially if they must be taken indoors for the winter, but might not be appropriate for windy sites. Chairs that stack or fold and tables that fold will minimize needed storage space.

above • Multiple dining spaces like these two areas are a plus if you host large dinner parties. They are also wonderful if you have children who like having a separate table for dining with their own friends.

above • Picnic tables are still as practical as they always were. And these days, they come in more styles, such as this one with straight legs and an oversize market umbrella for protection from the sun.

above • Scale is an important consideration when selecting a dining table and chairs. Anything smaller than this eight-person teak table with cushioned chairs would feel lost in this large patio and garden setting.

Quick-and-Easy Buffet Table

When you're just beginning to create your outdoor living area, entertaining a larger-than-usual crowd, or just want a little more flexibility in the way you arrange furniture, you can always put indoor tables, card tables, and even cafeteria-style folding tables to use for special occasions. Here, a quilted blanket was used to dress up an old picnic table. Color-coordinated accessories, including antique shutters, a candleholder, dinner plates, container plantings, and even a ceramic guinea hen, add the finishing touches to create an attractive buffet table.

Dining Furniture

Commercially available outdoor dining sets come in an ever-increasing range of styles—from classic teak to sleek and stylish extruded aluminum. Many dining sets mix materials, such as tile-mosaic tabletops on iron, wood, or wicker frames. Round tables may feature a built-in lazy Susan, which is especially convenient when serving six or more people at a table. And it's entirely possible to build your own tables and chairs by using landscaping materials such as timber posts and stone in creative ways.

1. After dinner at this woven table for 10, guests can relax in the pool house or in one of several casual seating areas around the water. 2. These large stone slabs—several of which were salvaged when the swimming pool was being dug—were fashioned into a one-of-a-kind picnic table. 3. With its comfortably cushioned chairs, this dining table was positioned for ample sunshine and enticing views all day, from breakfast to lunch to dinner. The cushions establish a color scheme for the table settings.

A Tropical Dining Island

In this suburban neighborhood just north of Miami, where temperatures are warm (if not downright hot) year-round, water is an essential element of almost any backyard landscape. Most often, that means a swimming pool. But in this contemporary backyard, the owners expanded on that theme—adding a wall fountain and a tropical dining island surrounded by a canal.

In a playful way, the canal brings to mind a castle moat. But this canal is less than 2 ft. deep, filled with goldfish, and inviting rather than disarming. Though the water looks black, it's not—that's just the color in which the interior walls were finished. The water itself is clear, and the fish can be seen and enjoyed by the homeowners when they dine beneath the palm trees.

above • The contemporary styling of the ceramic and teak dining set complements this south Florida residence. The dark canals and light tile echo the dark windows and light exterior of the home.

above • The water feature defines this outdoor dining room, creating an island-like atmosphere beneath the palm trees in the backyard.

above • Large stone slabs, which are available in local stoneyards or from landscape contractors, make interesting rustic tabletops. This one sits on a rugged handmade wooden base that matches the nearby pavilion.

left • Tables with patterned-tile tops call for simple accessories. The natural-colored chair cushions, solid-colored plates, and simple vase of foliage are perfect accents that allow the tabletop to be the focal point.

Table Settings

Indoor tableware is fine outdoors, but it can be fun to experiment with a whole new color scheme or style for your open-air room. Because the setting is more casual, you can be more playful with outdoor table settings. Discount stores, flea markets, and antiques stores offer mix-and-match pieces at very affordable prices. While shopping, seek out candleholders, serving baskets, one-of-a-kind serving dishes, and fabric remnants for cloth napkins. Colorful melamine dishes or basket-style paper-plate holders are also practical choices for outdoor settings. And, finally, don't forget the centerpiece. Pick whatever is fresh in the garden that day—whether it's a bouquet of flowers, a bundle of foliage, or a bowl of sweet and juicy berries.

1. Tablecloths are an inexpensive way to change the look of table settings from one evening to another. Here, the homeowner chose a muslin that blends well with the antique serving baskets and bowls as well as with the landscape. 2. For a beach-themed pool party, shells and starfish add a fun accent to a tray of appetizers. 3. On a neutral-colored table, rich colors bring even the simplest table settings to life. This combination has a Spanish flair. 4. For an outdoor table, consider creating a color theme based on a natural centerpiece—such as this basket of locally grown green apples.

DESIGNING

The kitchen itself is just one piece of the puzzle.

No matter how big the grill or functional the cabinets,

AN OUTDOOR

you won't spend time outdoors unless you create a

comfortable space in which to relax with friends and family.

ROOM

Anatomy of an Outdoor Room

The concept of outdoor rooms evolved from the prac-
tice of dividing a garden into distinct spaces—an herb
garden, a rose garden, a courtyard garden, or an entry
garden. This simple act of division has the almost magical ability to make small gardens feel larger and large
landscapes more manageable. It also gives each space a
special role or design theme that can be explored cre-
atively. Outdoor rooms are similar, except that we tend
to think of them as spaces for activities such as cooking,
dining, relaxing, gardening, and recreation.

When it comes to designing outdoor rooms, most of the
terminology is very familiar to us—floors, ceilings, walls,
windows, passageways, furnishings, lighting, and accents.
However, while we may think and talk in terms of *rooms*
because they are familiar to us, it's important to remember
that outdoor rooms are just that—outdoors. As a result, the
design is looser, the materials are different, and the character of the space can change dramatically throughout
the seasons and even over the course of a day as the sun
moves across the sky.

Because outdoor rooms are exposed to the elements, they
get dirtier than indoor rooms. Yet the last thing most of
us want is another room to clean. So create your room
primarily with landscaping materials that will wear well;
look natural outdoors; and can be cleaned with a broom,
blower, or garden hose. Choose materials that, if they get
scratched or dinged, just take on more character. Accessories such as candles, vases, and tableware are fun to set
out when dining or entertaining, but elements you would
expect to find in a garden—such as container plantings,
sundials, sculpture, and fountains—will decorate your
open-air room year-round and should require only minimal care. The result will be a comfortable and inviting
space in your own backyard, where you can breathe the
fresh air and enjoy the great outdoors.

above · This urban courtyard may be tiny, but it features a dining area, seating
area, small fountain, and lush gardens anchored by boxwoods and roses. The
stylish furnishings and antiques give it lots of character.

left • The arid southwestern climate and the shelter of this deep portico make it possible to use indoor furniture like this pine country table outdoors. The built-in benches along the walls are wide enough to stretch out for a nap on a lazy afternoon.

Designing an Outdoor Room

Floors
- stone, brick, tile
- decorative concrete
- concrete pavers
- gravel
- mulch
- living ground covers

Ceilings
- shade trees
- arbor or pergola
- umbrella or awning
- porch or portico roof
- pavilion or gazebo

Furnishings and Accents
- furniture
- water features
- sculpture
- statuary and sundials
- container plantings
- birdhouses
- outdoor kitchens
- lighting

Passageways
- gates
- arbors or arches
- paths or steps
- rows of plantings

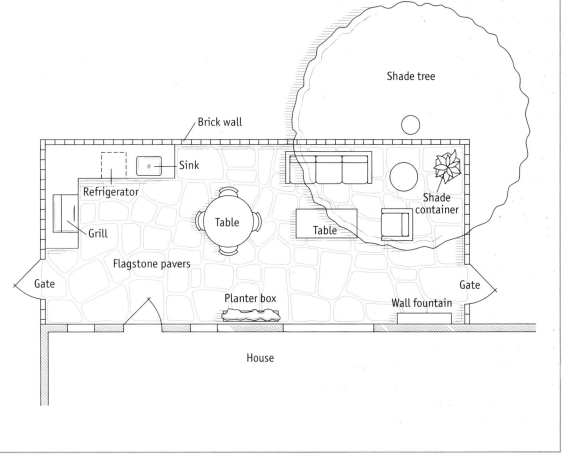

FLOORS

Inside a home, you typically design within a space. Outdoors, you have to create that space. And while you must conceive of the space as a whole in terms of its location, size, and style, you typically begin the construction process with the floors. Floors should be level; have a reasonably smooth, nonslip surface; drain well after a rain shower; and contribute to the overall character of the space.

The most practical choices for patios are stone, brick, concrete, and tile. Stone is available as irregular flagstone, cut pavers, granite cobbles, pea gravel, and granite fines. Brick is a very uniform building material and is available in a range of colors and sizes (from full-size bricks to thin pavers). Among tile, the most durable choices are porcelain and stone, as they show less wear and won't crack during the freeze–thaw cycle. The concrete we thought we knew has now grown up. In its many new forms—including stained, etched, stamped, and formed into pavers—it ranks among the most versatile of patio flooring materials. Some of the most interesting floors are those that mix two or three different materials or display materials in unique patterns. Mortared stone, brick, and pavers have a more refined look, but dry laid, they show a wonderful rustic character and allow rainwater to soak into the ground fairly easily.

Decks come with their own range of materials, many of them also new. In addition to pressure-treated pine, cedar, and redwood—the standards for many years—natural-wood choices now include tropical hardwoods such as ipe, teak, and mahogany. Several alternative decking materials valued for their longer life spans and lower maintenance requirements have also been introduced, including vinyl, vinyl-coated steel, plastic, and composite materials made of plastic and wood.

Personalized Paving

Perhaps the greatest characteristic of concrete is its malleability. You can stain it, score it, mix in aggregate for texture, or sprinkle sand on it before it dries for a rough surface. You can buy it in pavers of all shapes and sizes, or even have it stamped so that it looks like brick, stone, or tile if you like. These homeowners personalized their concrete—imprinting the floor of their outdoor kitchen with, appropriately enough, kitchen utensils before the concrete had a chance to set.

above • Like all-weather wicker furniture, all-weather outdoor rugs are a fairly recent introduction. This rug has been placed on the patio to help define the dining area and to break up the repetitive pattern of the paving.

facing page • How paving materials are laid is as important as which materials are selected. Here, brick pavers and irregular flagstone have been set in an intricate pattern with a band that resembles a colorful, patterned rug.

right • Tile mosaics usually require more patience than skill to lay, but they're worth the effort. This section of paving is accompanied by an equally detailed vignette of plants, stones, and tiny sculptures that encourage close inspection.

Floors

Outdoor floors can serve as a nondescript foundation for your outdoor kitchen and living areas or become a focal point for your outdoor room. Darker, solid-colored materials will tend to recede as a background material, whereas lighter-colored or mixed materials will demand more attention. Paving materials should complement your home's architecture, look at home in the landscape, and be durable in your local conditions.

STONE
$$–$$$

- Types include flagstone, cut-stone, cobbles, gravel, and fines
- Looks natural in the landscape
- Extremely durable
- Can be dry laid or mortared

BRICK
$$

- Available as full-size bricks or thin pavers
- Can relate well to architecture of the house
- Can be dry laid or mortared
- Durable
- Can get slippery in damp, shady sites

TILE
$$

- Porcelain and stone tile are best outdoor choices
- Many shapes, colors, and sizes
- Can relate well to architecture of the house
- Durable

CONCRETE
$

- Available with decorative finishes or as pavers
- Can be made to look like other materials
- Better choice for moderate climates than for cold climates

WOOD
$–$$

- Treated pine, cedar, redwood, and tropical hardwoods are weather resistant
- Blends in with the landscape
- Durability and life span vary

COMPOSITE DECKING
$$

- Most use recycled materials
- Lower maintenance, longer lifespan than wood
- Most don't look natural
- Provides good traction

PLASTIC AND METAL DECKING
$$–$$$

- Available in vinyl, vinyl-coated steel, and plastic
- Lightweight, but durable
- Lower maintenance, longer lifespan than wood
- Most don't look natural

PORCELAIN TILE

FLAGSTONE AND STONE TILE

COMPOSITE DECKING

CONCRETE PAVERS

WALLS, WINDOWS, AND PASSAGEWAYS

The walls of an outdoor room may be real or implied. A stone wall, board privacy fence, or dense hedge, for instance, is not easily penetrated either visually or physically. A pierced-brick wall, iron fence, or loosely planted screen may prevent passage, but can certainly been seen through. And with a pergola, the posts supporting the overhead beams define its walls, even if no physical walls are present. Other types of walls are vine-covered trellises, house walls, rows of containers, and low seat walls.

Beyond contributing to the structure of an outdoor room, walls can provide screening from neighbors, passing cars, or undesirable views. They may serve as a visual backdrop to an outdoor kitchen and furnishings or provide a physical barrier—especially if your outdoor room includes a swimming pool. Although any wall's height should be in scale with the room, taller walls tend to create cozier settings and low walls create an airy atmosphere. Their surfaces may be a solid and smooth or more tapestry-like. They should enhance, rather than compete with, the other elements in an outdoor room.

Like walls, passageways can also be real or implied. A gate provides a physical door that opens, closes, and may even lock. Yet a 4-ft. opening in a hedge or stone wall is no less a passageway. Two posts, a pair of large containers, an arbor, or even the arched branch on a tree may serve as a entryway. Paths, hedges, or narrow pergolas may form hallways. And steps or grade changes in terraces can mark the transition from one space to another.

Unless they are built into a pavilion or other structure, outdoor "windows" are almost always open. They may be gaps built into masonry walls, spaces cut into hedges, or framed openings in a trellis.

above • The clean lines of a bamboo arbor frame the entrance to this secret garden room, where comfortable seating and refreshments await friends for relaxed conversation or perhaps a couple intent on spending the afternoon reading.

Creating a Seat Wall

Seat walls are an attractive option when you define an area but don't want to block the view. Built 14 in. to 16 in. high, they are the perfect height for sitting. While it might not be comfortable to sit on a masonry wall for very long, it's just right for short-term or overflow seating when hosting a party—especially a casual cookout or cocktail buffet. Although it isn't always necessary, most seat walls have a capstone made from a smooth-surfaced, cut stone that is 1½ in. to 2 in. thick and at least 12 in. wide. This provides a broad surface for sitting that won't snag clothing and gives the wall a finished look. Bluestone slabs are a favorite choice because they have a smooth finish and look good with brick, stucco, and many other stones.

right • A classic arbor and open gates issue a welcoming invitation to guests arriving for a dinner party at this poolside pavilion. Stepping-stones, which offer a sense of intrigue, lead from the driveway to the pool deck.

below • Hedges form a dense, evergreen wall to create a sense of privacy in this outdoor room. A simple gap in the hedge serves as a doorway—both framing the view and providing a point of entry.

Walls

Walls can be short or tall, impenetrable or see-though, permanent or ever changing. They can serve as a focal point in an outdoor room or as a solid, unobtrusive backdrop for plantings or decorative elements. And they can be designed to tie in with the home's architecture or to blend almost seamlessly into the surrounding landscape.

FENCE
$$
- Available in wood, iron, metal, or composite materials
- Styles can blend with architecture
- Width and spacing of pickets determine screening
- May require regular maintenance
- Many styles available

MASONRY WALL
$$$
- Choices include stone, brick, or stucco
- Can provide immediate screening and barrier
- Can blend with landscape or architecture
- Extremely durable and long lasting

SEAT WALL
$$–$$$
- Can be created from stone, stucco, or brick
- Doesn't provide screening but does provides a place to sit
- Can blend with landscape and architecture
- Extremely durable and long lasting

TRELLIS
$
- Created in lattice or similar structure
- Structure can be seen through without vines
- Screening vines take time to grow in
- Requires maintenance, and vines need to be pruned

LIVING WALL
$
- Created from hedge or mixed plantings
- Takes time to establish
- Provides a living, textural backdrop
- Blends into the landscape
- Requires periodic care
- Provides a habitat for birds

WOOD FENCE

OPEN-WEAVE TRELLIS

STUCCO WALL

CEILINGS

The ceiling of an outdoor room can be tied into the style of your home, particularly if one or more of the rooms are located close to the house, but it is often dictated by local climate. A solid roof over at least part of the outdoor cooking, dining, or entertaining areas is almost essential where unexpected rain showers are common. In cooler parts of the country, a ceiling of blue sky and sunshine may be most desirable. In the hot, dry Southwest, some shelter from the sun—whether a shade tree, pergola, portico, or umbrella, is usually a necessity. But space permitting, almost any outdoor living area can benefit from a mix of ceiling types to provide a choice of sun, shade, or more protective shelter as the light and conditions change or as moods warrant. These more vertical accents also make an outdoor living area more visually interesting.

ADDING YOUR PERSONALITY AND STYLE

The fun part of designing an outdoor room is putting your personal imprint on the space. Regardless of location, outdoor spaces are meant to be fun and relaxed; and because the materials available for creating these spaces are so varied, this is a wonderful opportunity to experiment with colors, textures, and styles.

There are many places to seek inspiration. The vernacular landscape is a good starting point: Landscapes in Santa Fe, Miami, Boston, and Denver, for instance, each has its own unique personality that is defined by indigenous building materials, native plants, and local history. But it's also possible to draw inspiration from childhood memories, favorite travels, or other cultures. For some, it's all about texture and earthy materials. For others, color is the most expressive design element. Something as simple as the fabric for seat cushions can inspire an entire color scheme for an outdoor room.

right • Bright, tropical colors set the mood for a festive afternoon beneath this gazebo. As the sun begins to sink, the flickering candle-light chandelier will contribute a romantic note. Island music and frozen drinks would add the finishing touches for a special occasion.

above • This classically styled arbor creates a ceiling over the dining area, which is adjacent to a seating area with hearth and outdoor kitchen (to right). The white accessories, white roses, and white posts pull the space together.

left • Shadows cast by this broad, attached arbor change throughout the day as the sun moves across the sky. Facing south, the patio receives sunshine all day, so the shade of the arbor is especially appreciated in the heat of summer.

171

Almost Like a Day at the Beach

He had renovation experience and a lifelong passion for architecture. She was an interior designer. So it was natural that they would design their own pool house—a modest structure with clean lines and built for entertaining—and serve as general contractors for the project. The gathering area is open to the pool, but bamboo shades can be dropped for protection in inclement weather and in the winter. A half bath with space to change clothes anchors one end of the building, while a kitchenette with a sink, prep counter, under-counter refrigerator, and serving bar occupies the other end.

One of the owners grew up along the coast of Florida and, when going through some family things, came across several ladies' swimsuits from the 1950s and 1960s. These swimsuits (which hang on the changing-room wall) inspired a beach decorating theme that has been carried throughout the pool house with buoys, shells, starfish, and a collection of mermaid memorabilia—including a full-size, tile-mosaic mermaid created by a local artist and installed for the homeowner's 40th birthday party.

In warm weather, the pool house stays busy. The family's teenage daughter loves hanging out at the pool with friends. Extended-family gatherings are hosted here to celebrate summer birthdays. Small, casual dinner parties are common on Friday and Saturday nights. There's a grill on the pool deck as well as a small dining table beneath an arbor, but everyone migrates to the pool house, where they're just as content holding their plates or eating from trays while sitting in more comfortable chairs. The bar counter is perfect for serving both food and drinks; and a set of colorful, nonbreakable dishes are stored on open shelving—an old baker's rack that hangs on the wall above the sink.

right • The serving bar is a simple, open-back structure that features a graceful curve for visual interest. For some events, it serves as a bar. For others, it's a buffet counter covered with platters.

above • The small kitchen has a sink, plenty of counter space for food preparation, several electrical outlets, and lots of storage space both above and below the counter. An under-counter refrigerator is located nearby, tucked beneath the serving bar.

left • The solid roof means a mix of indoor and outdoor furnishings could be used. A pair of antique wooden brackets support a board shelf. Atop this shelf a full-size tile-mosaic mermaid watches over the pool and attends all parties.

below • The pool house is an open-air structure designed to look out over the swimming pool. Windows on the rear wall, along with several ceiling fans, help circulate the air on hot summer evenings.

Lighting

Landscape lighting should be subtle, not bold. Unlike indoors, where lights reflect off walls to provide even illumination, outdoor lights quickly draw attention to whatever is being illuminated and away from other elements in the landscape. Also, outdoor lights can be seen from surprising distances—which neighbors or passersby might find distracting. For this reason, it is important to use only as much light as necessary and to light areas on a selective basis rather than illuminating an entire backyard.

There are two basic types of outdoor lighting: functional and accent. Functional lighting helps you move about safely after dark and tackle specific tasks. Lights that help you traverse steps or grill your dinner are good examples of functional lighting. Accent lighting is more about creating mood and ambience. It is also used to highlight certain elements in the landscape, such as a sculpture, a water feature, or even a tree with a unique branching habit. As a general rule, outdoor kitchens need more functional or task lighting, and dining and entertaining areas benefit most from accent lighting.

Outdoor living areas are best illuminated with several different types and intensities of light. Downlights hung from trees can provide soft overall lighting, whereas a chandelier and candles over a dining table add subtle yet focused light; a task lamp on the grill puts more intense light where needed; and path lights, either hardwired to the electrical system or low-voltage types, make it easy to move among the house, patio, and areas of the landscape.

top right • Hanging lanterns illuminate the outdoor kitchen and dining areas beneath the portico as well as a casual seating area between the house and the pool deck. Candles are placed on the tables for meals, and softer lights are used around the water.

right • Exterior house walls provide a solid surface for hanging outdoor fixtures and enable indoor wiring to be tapped. This wall lantern provides a soft, but broad glow that provides general illumination in a 10-ft. to 15-ft. arc.

Lighting Installation and Maintenance

Installing landscape lighting requires digging holes and trenches, and often involves installing lights in walls, decks, or arbors, so the best time to finalize a lighting plan is long before construction begins on any outdoor kitchens or patio. Despite the many do-it-yourself landscape lighting kits on the market (which are geared for paths), most outdoor living areas benefit from more sophisticated lighting schemes and higher-quality lighting fixtures than a homeowner can install without an electrician's license and training in lighting design. If you're investing in anything other than the simplest outdoor kitchen, consider consulting a professional lighting designer or landscape architect. As for maintenance, keep in mind that outdoor lights are exposed to the elements. They can easily get caked in dirt and knocked out of position. Inspect them at least annually for any needed adjustments, repairs, and bulb replacement.

above · Torches come in a wide range of styles such as this one made from blown glass, and can be positioned around a pool deck, patio, or pathway to create a festive atmosphere for entertaining.

left · These torch pots contain tins of proprietary gel that provide a long-burning source of fuel. Here, they are used around a swimming pool, though they can be placed in any low-traffic area of the landscape.

Types of Outdoor Lighting

Within the two basic categories of landscape lighting—functional and accent—there are numerous more specific types of lighting that apply to outdoor environments. Thinking through these categories can help you determine what types of lighting may work best in which locations.

GENERAL LIGHTING
- Provides overall illumination for a porch, patio, or deck
- Broad beam coverage
- Best when placed high—in a tree, on a wall, or on a pergola
- Allows light to fall softly on an area

TASK LIGHTING
- Sheds light on a specific task
- Narrow beam coverage
- Usually placed above the work or activity area
- Light can be bright but narrowly focused

PATH AND STEP LIGHTING
- Illumination covers paths and steps
- Broad beam coverage
- Usually placed within a couple of feet of the path or step
- Light is usually soft—just enough to safely move about
- Commonly mounted on low walls or short posts

ACCENT LIGHTING
- Used to highlight fountains, sculpture, trees, or other features
- Narrow beam coverage, often from two directions
- Fixtures frequently placed on or in the ground
- Light may be the brightest in the landscape

AMBIENT LIGHTING
- Used to create mood
- Provided by low, soft, and often flickering lights
- Limited coverage area
- Fixtures may be placed anywhere desired
- Usually the softest light in the landscape
- May include candles, torches, string lights, and other soft lights

ACCENT LIGHTS HUNG IN TREE AND REFLECTING IN POOL

BUILT-IN PATH LIGHT

TABLETOP TASK LIGHTING

GENERAL LIGHTING OVER AN EATING AREA

Outdoor Lighting

Lighting is one of the most creative and complex elements in designing an outdoor room. Some of the secrets to creating effective outdoor lighting include mastering the art of subtlety, using light to draw the eye where you want it to go, and mixing and matching different types of lights and fixtures effectively. The more control you have over individual fixtures, the better. Individual switches and dimmer controls allow you to adjust the lights as you shift from cooking to dining, or to tone them down as the evening winds down.

1. A candle chandelier makes it possible to light a dining table without electricity. 2. These decorative string lights provide soft illumination in an outdoor kitchen when the overhead lights are off. 3. Lanterns look great hanging from tree limbs and provide protection for the candles. 4. Short torches placed in container plantings accent a swimming pool cascade and provide gentle illumination around the pool's edge.

Outdoor Hearths

On a cool evening, nothing attracts a crowd like a fire. Whether it's a portable fire dish or custom-built fireplace, both the flickering flames and radiating heat draw like magnets. Fire pits, available as portable units or permanently installed, are especially suitable for social gatherings, as friends can gather around them for hours of easy conversation, just as they would around an old-fashioned campfire. Fireplaces create an ambience more akin to a family room, encouraging guests to relax in nearby chairs facing the fire or perhaps to take turns sitting on the hearth. The warmth provided by a fireplace can knock the chill off a cool evening and help extend the season for outdoor living—although it's important to keep in mind that an outdoor hearth won't heat an open space the same way it will an enclosed space. The heat simply dissipates too quickly.

Custom-built fireplaces and fire pits can require a substantial investment but can make an equally substantial architectural impact in any outdoor room. More affordable types of both are ready-made for immediate installation and come in a growing range of styles and materials. The most popular outdoor hearths are the portable chimineas, fire pits, fire dishes, and luminaries that can be easily moved about the patio or from one home to another. For those more interested in the heat than the ambience, a patio heater is a practical alternative. Like those used in outdoor restaurants, they come in floor, tabletop, and wall-mounted models.

In addition to wood and natural gas, fireplaces can be fueled with liquid propane, manufactured logs, and proprietary gels. If you're building a wood-burning fireplace, don't forget to designate a convenient space for wood storage as well as a set of fireplace tools and perhaps a grate or pot crane that will allow you to cook over the fire.

right • Oversize fireplaces work well outdoors. This large wood-burning fireplace dominates and sets the tone for a rustic dining patio. The picnic table, twig chairs, and dry-laid stone floor help carry out the theme.

right • Along with the built-in benches on either side, this gas fireplace forms a wall along one edge of the sheltered outdoor room and is a focal point as you approach from the house.

below • The brick fireplace anchors a small patio, creating a cozy seating area for six. It also creates a dividing wall between this room and the dining area located beneath the pergola.

above • This stone fire pit was affordable and relatively easy to build; only basic masonry skills were needed to mortar the stones together. Because it doesn't need access to gas lines, the wood-burning pit can be built in a destination garden setting.

Outdoor Hearths

When it comes to choosing an outdoor hearth, it's important to know whether your needs are more about warming up a space or creating ambience and to select an option that is in scale with the space. Fireplaces and fire pits add plenty of atmosphere; but for the limited space they occupy, patio heaters can put out more heat. And while portable hearths are ideal for small spaces, they can look lost on a large patio.

PORTABLE FIRE DISHES
$

- Styles include fire dish, chiminea, fire pit, and luminaria
- Great for small spaces
- Can be easily moved

MANUFACTURED FIREPLACES AND FIRE PITS
$$

- Ready-made, freestanding models
- Many styles available
- Lightweight construction, so it can be delivered to site

CUSTOM-BUILT FIREPLACES AND FIRE PITS
$$$

- Built on site to your specifications
- Materials can be selected to match surroundings
- Heavy-duty, permanent installation

PATIO HEATERS
$$

- Limited range in styles but includes floor, tabletop, and wall-mount models

FIREPLACE WITH GAS STARTER

NATURAL-GAS FIRE PIT

PORTABLE WOOD-BURNING CHIMINEA

GAS PATIO HEATER

Fireplaces

Fireplaces and fire pits are available for just about any location—whether on a patio or deck, beneath a pavilion, or in a woodsy retreat. As always when dealing with fire, take appropriate safety precautions to make sure there's nothing flammable overhead and that any portable units placed on decks are specifically designed for that use.

1. The fireplace gives this small backyard patio a reason for existing. The flanking seat walls anchor the patio in the landscape and provide a place to take a rest without blocking views of the lake. 2. Built into the wall of a circular patio, this rectangular fire pit burns either wood or charcoal. It's ideal for roasting marshmallows, and a cooking grate can be placed on top of the bricks for grilling. 3. Although it is located just below a more formal outdoor kitchen and dining area on a sloping lot, this fire pit provides a peaceful camp-style setting. 4. A platform with wraparound seating was built to accommodate this decorative fire pit. It doubles as a table with room to set down plates or drinks. 5. A portable fire dish adds personality and warmth in even the smallest gathering spaces—such as this small garden niche that has just enough room for two.

Fireplace Anchors an Outdoor Room

Inside a home, friends gather in the kitchen or near a fireplace. The same holds true outdoors— especially when the kitchen and fireplace reside side by side. In this case, that combination packs a powerful one-two punch that makes this poolside gathering space the ideal place for entertaining outdoors. But it's not just the combination of elements that works. It's also the way they are pieced together. The grilling island and fireplace are both physically and visually connected by distinctive redwood trellising and a built-in stone bench. A second stone bench extends from the opposite side of the fireplace.

Another unique feature of this outdoor kitchen and fireplace combo is the gentle inward arc that it forms, warmly embracing the seating and dining areas. The fireplace, benches, and two trellises were skillfully built along this arc. The ironwork and candelabras over the fireplace are pieces the owners found in their travels; the stonemason created a shallow alcove so the ironwork would fit flush with the fireplace stone.

The generously proportioned fireplace is based on centuries-old plans drawn by Count Rumford that are still in use today. The design is noted for its ability to draw and reflect heat especially well. The designer uses these plans as the basis for all of her fireplace designs, and says she has never been disappointed in their performance.

right • The fireplace is generously proportioned to match the scale of the surrounding landscape, with its large, mature trees and broad, open lawns. The height of the hearth is lower than that of the benches, which adds dimension to the design.

above • The curve of the fireplace and stone benches is subtle but striking. Even the wood in the trellis has been skillfully crafted to echo the curve. The arc was laid out on site using a small stake, string, and chalk.

above • This outdoor kitchen and hearth combo includes a pellet grill and Rumford-style fireplace that is designed to draw well and reflect lots of heat. There's ample room on the patio for dining and relaxing.

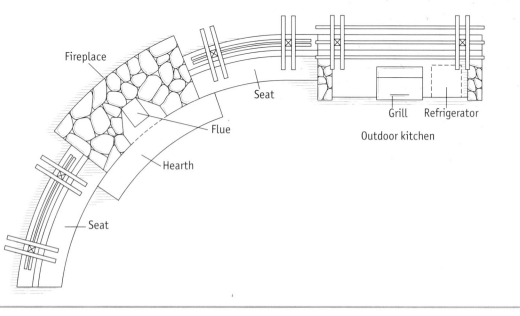

Fireplace

Seat

Flue

Hearth

Grill   Refrigerator

Outdoor kitchen

Seat

Outdoor Furniture

Patio furniture isn't what it used to be. Today's choices rival those of indoor furniture for comfort and style. It's just one more way in which the lines between indoors and out have been blurred. But outdoor furniture has to be ruggedly built so that woods won't rot, metals won't rust, and fabrics won't fade or mildew. And even though some outdoor furniture collections would look equally at home indoors, there is still a strong sense of outdoor style that remains popular and appropriate in most outdoor furnishings.

In addition to long-time favorites such as teak, cedar, wrought-iron, and molded plastic, choices for outdoor furniture now include exotic woods like ipe and mahogany, all-weather wicker and rattan, enamel-coated steel, cast aluminum, and galvanized metal dipped in a zinc bath. Some new materials are even made to look like their heavier, higher-maintenance, or more-expensive cousins: Powder-coated cast aluminum looks like wrought iron, but is lighter weight and won't rust. Adirondack chairs made from recycled plastic containers look remarkably like wood but don't have to be painted and won't rot. Mixed materials are popular, too. Wood tables look great with woven chairs, while woven seats complement metal frames. Sling-style fabric seats make wooden chairs more comfortable. Stone slabs make stunning tabletops when paired with a wooden or stone base. And fabric cushions almost always soften any solid-surface frame.

When shopping for furniture, start by choosing durable materials that won't easily rot, rust, stain, splinter, peel, or fade outdoors. Pieces should be heavy enough so they won't blow over on a windy day, but light enough that they can be easily rearranged. Of utmost importance is the comfort test: Always sit in a chair, sofa, or bench before you buy. And while you obviously want a style that suits your outdoor kitchen, outdoor room, and home in general, keep in mind that simple is often better than ornate in an outdoor environment where there's already so much going on visually.

right • More manufacturers are offering mixed-material furniture than ever before. This dining set features a cast-aluminum table base and chairs with fabric cushions and a mixed-tile tabletop.

Weather-Worthy Fabrics

Standard upholstery fabrics don't weather well outdoors—they fade, mildew, and disintegrate in short order. Yet there are new, weather-resistant fabrics made from acrylic, polyester, and vinyl mesh that rival cottons, silks, linens, and jacquards for their colors, patterns, and textures. They dry quickly, resist fading, and are easy to clean.

Outdoor cushions are different, too. Although cotton stuffing has been the standard, polyurethane foam and polyester fiber have proven to be more suitable for outdoor use. Polyester fiber dries more quickly, but polyurethane foam holds its shape better and lasts longer.

Despite these improvements, cushions still take more abuse than their sturdier frames. To extend the lifespan of outdoor cushions, store them indoors during winter and spot-clean fabrics with mild soap and warm water. For tough stains, use a fabric stain remover.

above • Rustic twig furniture is still a popular and stylish choice for outdoor settings. However, it must be treated with a sealer at least once a year to prevent rotting if exposed to the elements.

left • Adirondack chairs are surprisingly comfortable, even without seat cushions. These were made from pressure-treated and painted lumber, though they are also available in recycled plastic and with natural finishes in rot-resistant hardwoods.

right • Teak is a classic choice for outdoor furniture. This chair is made from quality-grade lumber that should last decades—though it will, in time, weather to an attractive silvery gray unless sealed regularly.

Outdoor Furniture Materials

Like everything else around an outdoor kitchen, the furniture must be built to withstand local conditions. Water, extreme temperature swings, and extended exposure to sun can take their toll on even the best-designed outdoor furniture.

WOOD
$$–$$$

- Teak and other tropical hardwoods the most durable
- Redwood, cedar, cypress, and pressure-treated pine most affordable
- Classic looking; blends with the natural environment
- Sturdy—not easily blown by wind
- Doesn't get too hot or too cold
- Seek out pieces made from renewably farmed and fairly traded woods
- Often bulky or heavy
- Nontropical woods require regular coat of protectant
- Lasts 10 to 40 years, depending on wood type and care

IRON
$$

- Heavy, but sturdy
- Must be painted or powder-coated to prevent rust
- Many styles available
- Can get hot or cold, depending on weather
- Hard surface; cushions may be needed for comfort

ALUMINUM
$

- Doesn't rust, though it will whiten and pit
- Tubular aluminum is lightweight and inexpensive
- Solid aluminum is heavier and more diverse
- Can get hot or cold, depending on weather
- Hard surface; cushions may be needed for comfort

SHELL-BACK ADIRONDACK CHAIRS MADE FROM RECYCLED PLASTIC

WOVEN
$$

- Available as marine-varnished reeds, plastic-wrapped fiber, or acrylic strips
- Sturdy metal frame with comfortable woven cover
- Lasts up to 30 years
- Dries slowly after rain
- Comfortable with or without cushions

PLASTIC
$–$$

- Resin or recycled-plastic construction
- Light weight
- Easy to clean
- Often stackable
- Available in many colors

EXTRUDED-ALUMINUM CHAIRS

POWDER-COATED ALUMINUM DINING CHAIRS AND TABLE WITH GLASS TABLETOP

Types of Outdoor Seating

There are several categories of furniture unique to the outdoors. In addition to occasional chairs, sofas, love seats, and stools traditionally found indoors, options include wall seats, garden benches, chaise longues, hammocks, and porch swings. You may not find all of these in the same retail store, and seat walls have to be built on site, so it's important to think about what type of seating might best suit your needs before you go shopping.

SWINGS, ROCKERS, AND GLIDERS
$–$$

- Favorites for porches
- Traditional garden styling
- Movement is relaxing

BAR STOOLS
$–$$

- Come in several heights, so measure your bar
- Stools with backs and arms occupy more space than those without
- Some models swivel for easier access

CHAISE LONGUES
$$–$$$

- The favorite for sunbathing
- Comfortable for napping
- Perfect for pool decks
- Sometimes awkward in furniture groupings

CUSHIONED CHAIRS AND SOFAS
$$–$$$

- Rival indoor furniture for style and comfort
- Easy to mix and match for groupings
- Many finishes and fabrics available

GARDEN BENCHES
$–$$

- Traditional garden styling
- Easily placed in outdoor room or landscape
- Can be uncomfortable for extended seating

HAMMOCKS
$–$$

- Perfect for napping
- Must be hung on posts or a frame
- Occupies a lot of space
- Not very conducive to furniture groupings

CUSHIONED OCCASIONAL CHAIRS

CUSHIONED BARSTOOL

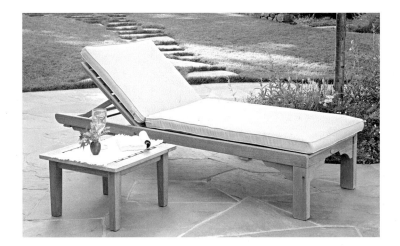

CUSHIONED LOUNGE CHAIR

BUILT-IN BENCH SEATING

Outdoor Seating Areas

It's fun to create multiple seating areas in a backyard. In spaces designed for entertaining, grouped seating with plush cushions will encourage guests to relax and stay a while. Dining areas will get lots of use placed near an outdoor kitchen. If there's someone special in your life, consider a romantic spot for two, perhaps overlooking a garden or other special view. Kids love having their own gathering spaces, too, with tables and chairs that fit them just right. And don't forget a quiet space just for one, where you can escape for a few moments on your own.

1. These lightweight, sling-back chairs can be easily moved to accommodate guests' seating preferences. 2. With all the seats facing each other, this furniture grouping is designed for easy conversation. 3. Chaise longues, including this double lounge under a large umbrella, have been positioned in several poolside groupings. They provide a variety of sun and shade options as the light changes throughout the day.

Accents and Accessories

While structural elements like patio floors, kitchen cabinets, and arbors may define an outdoor space and signify its style, it's often the accessories that give an outdoor room personality. Container plantings are a natural and obvious choice for outdoors. They can divide spaces, frame entries, decorate tabletops, bring life to an empty corner, or serve as a focal point against a wall. Fill them with fragrant flowers, colorful foliage plants, or even edible herbs and vegetables that can be snipped or harvested for meals.

Water features—from a small spouting fountain in a fishpond to a gently bubbling urn or trickling wall fountain—can bring a space to life like nothing else. In addition to helping create a soothing setting, the sound of moving water can help mask street and neighborhood noises. Statuary, sundials, and sculpture are all appropriate accessories for an outdoor room. The key to using such elements rests in their placement. A single striking piece often makes a stronger statement than multiple objects competing for attention—although it's possible to showcase multiple pieces by giving them their own space and limiting the number of pieces viewed from any one location. Place these ornaments among plantings, against a solid background such as a hedge or masonry wall, in a corner, or on a tabletop.

Other accessories to consider for an outdoor room include decorative outdoor lighting fixtures, colorful pillows, vases of fresh flowers, outdoor rugs, or even mirrors (which can make a space look larger). If you wish to create an energizing environment, seek out bright, colorful objects. But if a relaxing setting is preferred, keep things simple and choose textural objects with soft or natural colors. And finally, don't forget the music. The right tunes coming from a quality sound system can set the perfect tone for a successful dinner party beneath the stars.

above • Traditional teak benches, tables, and chairs are gathered beneath a large market umbrella to create a shady outdoor seating area. An assortment of objects, including a carved sandstone container and sphere, accent the table.

below • Rusted iron pieces found around farms and old homesteads have been fashioned into a one-of-a-kind chandelier and a pair of giant candlesticks. The candlesticks double as flower vases that are the perfect size for sunflowers.

left · Pillows add a splash of color in an outdoor room while softening a stone bench. The fabric colors coordinate will with nearby plantings as well as other pieces of furniture in an outdoor dining and living area.

below · A vignette of unique containers, garden implements, and sculptural iron rooster mark the passageway between a side-yard garden and backyard dining room. The odd number of elements and the various height makes the composition successful.

Ornaments and Art

Outdoor ornaments can be bought, made, found, or recycled. They run the gamut from garden statuary, indoor decor with outdoor durability, birdhouses and birdbaths to architectural fragments, sculpture, and mobiles. They may be mounted on a house or garden walls, placed in borders as focal points, clustered on tables to create vignettes, or hung from tree limbs and pergolas. Seek out objects that speak to you and convey your sense of style—whether classic, exuberant, or humorous. Just make sure they are weather worthy.

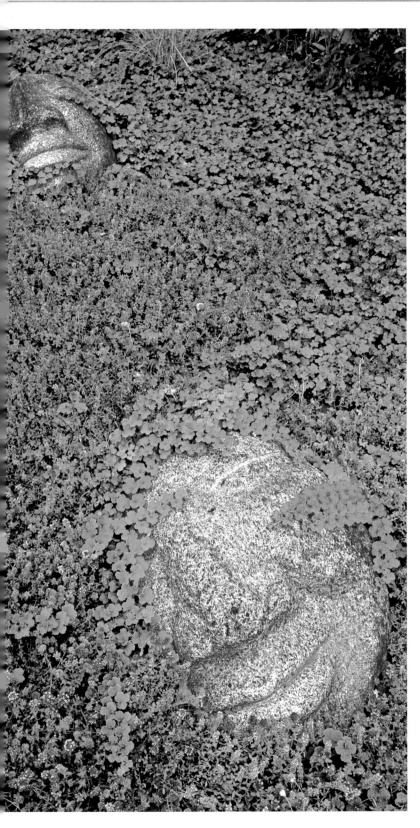

1. This ceramic fish swims through a sea of yellow salvia blossoms, showing how even small objects can make a big impression. 2. An old garden implement and ladder hang against the chimney, adding a sculptural accent to an outdoor dining area. 3. These carved-stone faces offer an element of surprise peering out from beneath a bed of thyme and creeping raspberry. 4. Found objects, like these stone fragments, make great conversation pieces.

Outdoor Media

There's nothing like a little Latin jazz to liven up the party or the soothing sound of classical music to set the tone for a romantic dinner. No matter what your musical preferences, a set of quality marine-grade speakers hooked to a stereo system will outperform a portable tabletop CD player. Directional-sound units (like those used indoors) are available in flush-mount, external-mount, or freestanding units. Some of the freestanding units feature cases that look like small boulders and can be placed discreetly in a garden bed. Another option is an intercom system featuring a built-in stereo speaker, which also provides the convenience of indoor–outdoor communication.

Outdoors, there are few walls to contain and bounce sound. So unless the area where you want music is fairly compact—such as a porch, pavilion, deck, or small patio—the sound dissipates quickly and there will be dead spots, where the sound simply gets lost. Small, omnidirectional speakers that offer 360-degree sound help solve this dilemma. A series of these speakers with slightly overlapping coverage areas (check the manufacturer's specifications for coverage) can often provide the most uniform sound coverage in a large backyard, around a swimming pool, in a garden, or even on a large deck. They can be mounted in ground, on ground, or on a hard surface such as a deck railing.

Outdoor televisions and home theaters are also available—making it easy to keep up with the game while grilling dinner or providing after-dinner entertainment. These feature all-weather enclosures, antiglare and scratch-resistant windows that protect the screen, and water-resistant remote controls. There are also oversize, inflatable screen systems that can turn a backyard into a drive-in theater.

top • Marine-grade speakers come in wall-mount, in-ground, and on-ground models. This is one of several positioned high on an exterior house walls near the pool and outdoor kitchen.

above • Conveniently located near the outdoor dining area, this speaker box features stereo and intercom controls. The intercom makes indoor–outdoor communication a snap—eliminating a few of those extra trips back to the kitchen.

above • This home theater was installed beneath the shelter of a portico where it could be viewed from the fireplace sitting area or the outdoor kitchen and bar. The shelter of the portico helps provide even lighting conditions for easy viewing.

Container Plantings

With or without plants, pots deserve a prominent place in any outdoor room. And chosen wisely, the containers can be just as interesting as any plants placed in them. But what's fun is matching the plants to the containers. Colored containers can inspire a complementary or contrasting planting scheme. Tall, narrow pots can be striking with a single plant cascading down its sides. Broad pots love bold foliage or multiple plants. Containers can be placed individually as focal points or clustered to create an entire garden from pots. Containers can also be moved around as flowers fade or foliage fills in.

1. This container inspired a color theme that includes plantings, architecture, and outdoor furniture. **2.** A simple grouping of three large pots filled with succulents adds life to an unused corner. **3.** Container plantings have been clustered around this deck to help define living, dining, and serving areas. **4.** Pots of foliage plants help soften the hard surfaces of this deck and transform an open patio into a series of smaller spaces.

Water Features

Whether you prefer a wall fountain as a focal point, a gently bubbling stone fountain tucked in a quiet corner, or a koi pond along the edge of the patio, there are water features adapted to every type of outdoor space. In addition to drawing the attention of guests, they'll also attract birds for your backyard enjoyment. The services of a landscape architect or contractor may be required for a large pond or fountain, but homeowners can install most small water features in a weekend. Some even come ready-made—just fill their basins with water and plug them in to the nearest GFCI (ground-fault circuit interrupter) outlet.

1. In hot climates, fountains are more common than fire pits—though they might occupy a similar space on a patio. 2. This self-contained fountain needed just water and an electricity source, so it was a snap to install. 3. Water spills over this bowl and through the rocks to a hidden underground basin that contains a recirculation pump. 4. The blue tiles make a strong visual connection between the patio floor and Mediterranean-style wall fountain. 5. The small bubbling stone suits this simply designed southwestern courtyard where days begin with a cup of coffee.

For new ideas and resources for outdoor living products and services, visit www.GardensAndLiving.com

Designers

CLEMENS & ASSOCIATES, INC.
www.clemensandassociates.com

DAVID THORNE LANDSCAPE ARCHITECTS
510-451-6161

DERVISS + CHAVEZ DESIGN + BUILD
www.dervissdesign.com

DESERT SAGE BUILDERS
www.dsbuild.com

FIRED UP KITCHENS
www.firedupkitchens.com

FOUR DIMENSIONS LANDSCAPE CO.
www.fourdimensionslandscape.com

P.O.P.S. LANDSCAPING
www.popslandscaping.com

SIMPLY OUTDOORZ
www.simplyoutdoorz.com

TWOMBLY NURSERY
www.twomblynursery.com

WATERCOLORS LLC
www.watercolorsonline.net

Specialty Outdoor Kitchen Companies

BAHAMA BLUE™
www.bahamablue.com

BARBECUES GALORE℠
www.bbqgalore.com

CALISE™ OUTDOOR KITCHEN CONCEPTS, INC.
www.outdoorkitchenconcepts.com

GRILL KITCHENS
www.grillkitchens.com

HEARTHSIDE FIREPLACE, PATIO AND BARBECUE CENTER
www.hearthsidedistributors.com

THE MAD HATTER
www.madhatterservices.com

OUTDOOR KITCHEN DISTRIBUTORS, INC.
www.outdoorkitchen.com

THE OUTDOOR KITCHEN STORE
www.outdoorkitchenstore.com

TEXAS PIT CRAFTERS
www.texaspitcrafters.com

TWIN EAGLES®
www.twineaglesbbq.com

Grilling Islands, Cabinets, and Countertops

CAL FLAME®
www.calspas.com

CAMBRIA®
www.cambriausa.com

DANVER
www.danver.com

DUPONT ®
www.zodiaq.com

GREEN MOUNTAIN SOAPSTONE®
www.greenmountainsoapstone.com

IN & OUT CABINETRY
www.outdoorkitchencabinetry.com

OUTDOOR KITCHENS
www.outdoorkitchens.com

OUTDOOR KITCHEN® COLLECTION
www.outdoorkitchencollection.com

SILESTONE®
www.silestoneusa.com

SIMPLY OUTDOORZ
www.simplyoutdoorz.com

WER/EVER OUTDOOR PRODUCTS
www.werever.com

Grills and Smokers

AMERICAN GRILLS
www.americangrills.com

BIG GREEN EGG®
www.biggreenegg.com

BIG JOHN GRILLS & ROTISSERIES
www.BigJohnGrills.com

BRINKMANN®
www.brinkmann.net

BROILKING®
www.broilkingbbq.com

BROILMASTER®
www.broilmaster.com

CHAR-BROIL®
www.charbroil.com

COOKSHACK®
www.cookshack.com

DCS™
www.dcsappliances.com/outdoor

DUCANE® GAS GRILLS
www.ducane.com

EVO®
www.evo-web.com

FIRE MAGIC®
www.firemagicgasgrills.com

FUEGO®
www.fuegoliving.com

GRILLS TO GO®
www.grillstogo.com

HEARTH, PATIO & BARBECUE ASSOCIATION℠
www.hpba.org

THE HOLLAND GRILL®
www.hollandgrill.com

KALAMAZOO OUTDOOR GOURMET
www.kalamazoogourmet.com

LYNX PROFESSIONAL GRILLS®
www.lynxgrills.com

MECO®
www.aussiegrill.com

PACIFIC GAS SPECIALTIES
www.pgscorp.com

THE PHOENIX GRILL CO.®
www.phoenixgrill.com

PRIMO GRILLS AND SMOKERS®
www.primogrill.com

SOLAIRE® INFRARED GRILLING SYSTEMS
www.solairegrills.com

TEC INFRA-RED GRILLS
www.tecinfrared.com

TRAEGER®
www.traegergrills.com

VIKING®
www.vikingrange.com

WEBER®
www.weber.com

Wood-Burning Ovens

EARTHSTONE® WOOD-FIRE OVENS
www.earthstoneovens.com

FOGAZZO®
www.fogazzo.com

FORNO BRAVO
www.fornobravo.com

GULATI INTERNATIONAL
www.tandoors.com

KALAMAZOO OUTDOOR GOURMET
www.kalamazoogourmet.com/pizza_
oven.php

MUGNAINI IMPORTS
www.mugnaini.com

SUPERIOR CLAY CORPORATION
www.superiorclay.com

Appliances and Accessories

BEVERAGE FACTORY
www.beveragefactory.com

COMPACT APPLIANCE
www.compactappliance.com

FAUCET.COM
www.faucet.com

FOOD SERVICE EQUIPMENT
www.fsega.com

FRANKLIN CHEF®
www.franklinchef.com

ICEANDWINE.COM
www.iceandwine.com
KITCHEN ACCESSORIES
www.rangehoods.com

MARVEL
www.lifeluxurymarvel.com

MPACT PRODUCTS (GRILL FLOSS™)
www.grillfloss.com

U-LINE CORPORATION®
www.u-line.com

Outdoor Hearth

BUCKLEY RUMFORD COMPANY
www.rumford.com

CALIFORNIA OUTDOOR CONCEPTS
www.californiaoutdoorconcepts.com

FIRE PIT SHOP
www.firepitshop.com

NEXO
www.nexofireplace.com

PATIO EMBERS®
www.patioembers.com

VERMONT CASTINGS®
www.myownbbq.com

Outdoor Lighting and Sound

BOSE®
www.bose.com

CRUTCHFIELD℠
www.crutchfield.com

GI DESIGNS
www.gidesigns.net

GRAND LIGHT LIGHTING AND DESIGN
www.grandlight.com

KICHLER® LIGHTING
www.kichler.com

LIGHTHOUSE LANDSCAPE LIGHTING℠
www.lightsbylighthouse.com

OUTDOOR LIGHTING PERSPECTIVES℠
www.outdoorlights.com

OUTDOOR MOVIES℠
www.outdoor-movies.com

SEA GULL LIGHTING®
www.seagulllighting.com

Outdoor Furniture

AUTHENTEAK™
www.authenteak.com

BROOKBEND OUTDOOR FURNITURE
www.brookbend.com

CALUCO
www.caluco.com

COUNTRY CASUAL®
www.countrycasual.com

FRONTGATE®
www.frontgate.com

HAUSER'S PATIO & RATTAN
www.hauserfurniture.com

KINGSLEY-BATE
www.kingsleybate.com

MAINE COTTAGE®
www.mainecottage.com

PATIO FURNITURE USA
www.patiofurnitureusa.com

PATIO LIVING & MORE
www.patiolivingandmore.com

PLOW & HEARTH®
www.plowhearth.com

RESTORATION HARDWARE℠
www.restorationhardware.com

SEASIDE CASUAL℠
www.seasidecasual.com

SMITH & HAWKEN℠
www.smithandhawken.com

SUNCOAST FURNITURE
www.suncoastfurniture.com

THOS. BAKER
www.thosbaker.com

TROPITONE®
www.tropitone.com

WESTMINSTER TEAK®
www.westminsterteak.com

WICKER ON PARK
www.wickeronpark.com

Paving and Decking Materials

CORRECTDECK®
www.correctdeck.com

DECK INFORMATION
www.decks.com

EVERGRAIN® COPMOSITE DECKING
www.evergrain.com

HANDYDECK
www.ezydeck.net

INTERNET LUMBER
www.internetlumber.com

LOCK DRY®
www.lockdry.com

PAVERSEARCH
www.paversearch.com

PAVESTONE®
www.pavestone.com

SWIFTDECK
www.swiftdeck.com

TIMBERTECH®
www.timbertech.com

TREX®
www.trex.com

UNILOCK®
www.unilock.com

Shade Structures

AMISH COUNTRY GAZEBOS®
www.amishgazebos.com

AWNING STORE
www.awningstore.com

AWNINGS.US
www.awnings.us

BALDWIN PERGOLAS
www.baldwinpergolas.com

DALTON PAVILIONS, INC.
www.daltonpavilions.com

GAZEBO CREATIONS™
www.gazebocreations.com

GAZEBO DEPOT
www.gazebodepot.com

ICON SHELTER SYSTEMS, INC.
www.iconshelters.com

JAVA PAVILIONS
www.javapavilions.com

LEISURE DESIGNS
www.leisuredesigns.com

LEISURE WOODS GAZEBOS
www.leisure-woods.com

OLD WORLD GAZEBOS®
www.gazebos.com

PARASOL FABRIC COVERED SHADE SHELTERS
www.portercorp.com

SAFARI™
www.safarithatch.com

SHADE SAILS
www.shadesails.com

SPIRIT ELEMENTS℠
www.spiritelements.com

SUMMERWOOD™ PRODUCTS
www.summerwood.com

VINYL PATIO KITS
www.vinylpatiokits.com

VIXEN HILL CEDAR PRODUCTS
www.VixenHill.com

CREDITS

pp. i–ii: Photos © Lee Anne White; design: Derviss + Chavez Design + Build

pp. iv–v: Photos (left to right) courtesy Seaside Casual; © Lee Anne White; design: Jon Carloftis; © Mark Lohman; © Lee Anne White; design: Enchantement Custom Builders; © Scot Zimmerman; courtesy Williams-Sonoma; © Mark Lohman; © Lee Anne White; design: Louise Poer; © Lee Anne White; design: Derviss + Chavez Design + Build; © Lee Anne White

p. vii: Photo courtesy Desert Sage Builders

p. viii: Photo © Scot Zimmerman

p. 2: Top photos (left to right) © Tim Street-Porter; Lee Anne White; design: Derviss + Chavez Design + Build; © Scot Zimmerman; © Anne Gummerson; © Lee Anne White; Eddie and Melissa Colvin residence; design: P.O.P.S. Landscaping; bottom photo © Tria Giovan

p. 3: Photo © Lee Anne White; Jones residence; design: P.O.P.S. Landscaping

CHAPTER 1

p. 4: Photo © Lee Anne White; design: David Feix

p. 6: © Scot Zimmerman

p. 7: (top) © Lee Anne White; Eddie & Melissa Colvin residence; design: P.O.P.S. Landscaping; (bottom) Brian Pontolilo, courtesy *Fine Homebuilding* magazine; design: Mary Jo Peterson

p. 8–9: © Lee Anne White; Roger & Lisa Davenport residence; design: P.O.P.S. Landscaping

p. 10: (top) © Lee Anne White; design: P.O.P.S. Landscaping; (bottom) © Lee Anne White; design: Four Dimensions Landscape Company

p. 11: © Scot Zimmerman

p. 12: © Lee Anne White; design: Derviss + Chavez Design + Build

p. 13: (top) © Lee Anne White; design: Derviss + Chavez Design + Build; (bottom) © Lee Anne White

p. 14: (top) © Lee Anne White; design: J.C. Enterprise Services; (bottom) © Lee Anne White; design: Derviss + Chavez Design + Build

p. 15: © Tim Street-Porter

p. 16: © www.carolynbates.com

p. 17: © Lee Anne White

p. 18: © Lee Anne White; design: Hillary Curtis, David Thorne Landscape Architects

p. 19: (top left) © Lee Anne White; design: Hillary Curtis, David Thorne Landscape Architects; (top right) Lee Anne White; design: Hillary Curtis, David Thorne Landscape Architects; (bottom) © Lee Anne White; design: Hillary Curtis, David Thorne Landscape Architects

p. 20: (top) © www.carolynbates.com; (bottom) © Saxon Holt

p. 21: © Lee Anne White; design: Betty Romberg

p. 22: (top) © Lee Anne White; design: P.O.P.S. Landscaping; (bottom) © Lee Anne White

p. 23: © Lee Anne White; design: P.O.P.S. Landscaping

p. 24: (top) © www.carolynbates.com; (bottom) © Lee Anne White; design: The Mad Hatter

p. 25: © Allan Mandell; design: Ron Wagner and Nani Waddoups

p. 26: © Ken Gutmaker; design: Dan Berger

p. 27: © Rick Keating, RK Productions; design: Bob Linnell

CHAPTER 2

p. 28: © Mark Lohman

p. 30: © Mark Turner

p. 31: (top) © Lee Anne White; design: Enchantment Custom Builders; (bottom) © Scot Zimmerman

p. 33: © Art Gray

p. 34: © Mark Lohman

p. 35: (top) © Scot Zimmerman; (bottom) © Lee Anne White; design: Jennifer Romberg Designs & Jane Taylor, Cottage Garden Antiques

p. 36: © Lee Anne White; design: Derviss + Chavez Design + Build

p. 37: (top and bottom) © Lee Anne White; design: Derviss + Chavez Design + Build

p. 38: (top) © Lee Anne White; (bottom) © www.carolynbates.com

p. 39: © Scot Zimmerman

p. 40: © Lee Anne White; design: P.O.P.S. Landscaping

p. 41: © Courtesy Franciscan Landscape Design

p. 42: (top) © Lee Anne White; Debbie and Larry Niffin residence; design: P.O.P.S. Landscaping; (bottom) © Lee Anne White; Debbie and Larry Niffin residence; design: P.O.P.S. Landscaping

p. 43: © Lee Anne White; Debbie and Larry Niffin residence; design: P.O.P.S. Landscaping

p. 45: © Anne Gummerson

pp. 46–47: © Lee Anne White; Timothy McComas residence; design: Desert Sage Builders

p. 49: © Lee Anne White; Desert Sage Builders

p. 50–51: © Lee Anne White; design: Watercolors

p. 53: © Scot Zimmerman

CHAPTER 3

p. 55: © Tim Street-Porter

p. 56: © Lee Anne White; design; Desert Sage Builders

p. 57: (top) © Anne Gummerson; (bottom) ©Lee Anne White; Judy Martine residence; design: Four Dimensions

p. 58: © Saxon Holt

p. 59: (top left) © Lee Anne White; design: Enchantment Custom Builders; (top right) © Lee Anne White; (bottom) © Lee Anne White; design: P.O.P.S. Landscaping

p. 60–62: © Lee Anne White

p. 63: (top & bottom left) © Lee Anne White; (bottom right) © www.carolynbates.com

p. 64: (top) © Lee Anne White; design: P.O.P.S. Landscaping; (bottom) © Lee Anne White

p. 65: © Lee Anne White; Grill courtesy Food Service Equipment

p. 66: (top) © Lee Anne White; design: Simply Outdoorz; (bottom) © Lee Anne White

p. 67: (top) © www.carolynbates.com; (bottom) © Lee Anne White

p. 68–69: © Lee Anne White; design: Derviss + Chavez Design + Build

p. 70: (top) © Lee Anne White; courtesy Barbecues Galore; (bottom) © Lee Anne White

p. 71: © Lee Anne White

p. 72: (top) © Lee Anne White; courtesy Barbecues Galore (bottom) © Lee Anne White

p. 73: © Lee Anne White

p. 74: (1) © Lee Anne White; design: Allied Kitchen & Bath; (2) © Lee Anne White; design: Desert Sage Builders; (3) © Lee Anne White

p. 75: (4) © Lee Anne White; (5) © Lee Anne White; design: Desert Sage Builders

p. 76: © Lee Anne White

p. 77: courtesy Williams-Sonoma

p. 78: © Lee Anne White

p. 79: (top) © Lee Anne White; courtesy Barbecues Galore (bottom) © Lee Anne White

p. 80: (top) © Lee Anne White; design: Fired Up Kitchens (bottom) © Alan Mandell; design: Ron Wagner and Nani Waddoups

p. 81: © Lee Anne White; design: Forno Bravo and Fired Up Kitchens

p. 82: © Scot Zimmerman

p. 83–85: © Lee Anne White; design: Forno Bravo and Fired Up Kitchens

CHAPTER 4

p. 86: © Lee Anne White; design: P.O.P.S. Landscaping

p. 88: © Lee Anne White

p. 89: (top) © Lee Anne White; design: Simply Outdoorz; (bottom) © Lee Anne White; Dr. & Mrs. Timothy McComas residence; design: Desert Sage Builders

p. 90: (top)© Mark Lohman; (bottom) © Lee Anne White; design: Simply Outdoorz

p. 91: © Lee Anne White

p. 92–93: © Lee Anne White; design: Chris & Alison Romberg; courtesy Food Service Equipment

p. 94: (top) © Lee Anne White; John & Abby Hoffman residence; design: Derviss + Chavez Design + Build; (bottom) © Lee Anne White; design: Simply Outdoorz

p. 95: © Lee Anne White

p. 96: (1) © Scott Zimmerman; (2) © Lee Anne White; design: Chris & Alison Romberg

p. 97: (3) © Lee Anne White; (4) © Lee Anne White; design: J.C. Enterprise Services; (5) © Lee Anne White; design: Jennifer Romberg Designs & Jane Taylor/Cottage Garden Antiques

p. 98: (top) © Lee Anne White; courtesy Barbecues Galore; (bottom)

© Lee Anne White; Roger & Lisa Davenport residence; design: P.O.P.S. Landscaping

p. 99: (top) © Lee Anne White; design: Hillary Curtis, David Thorne Landscape Architects; (bottom) © Lee Anne White; design: Fired Up Kitchens

p. 100–101: © Lee Anne White; design: Simply Outdoorz

p. 102: (1 and 2) Lee Anne White

p. 103: (3 and 4) © Lee Anne White; (5) © Lee Anne White; courtesy Food Service Equipment

p. 104: © Lee Anne White; design: Derviss + Chavez Design + Build

p. 105: (top) © Lee Anne White; design: Simply Outdoorz; (bottom) © Lee Anne White; Susan & Arnie Zisselman residence; design: Allied Kitchen & Bath

p. 106: © Lee Anne White; design: Simply Outdoorz

p. 107: (top) © Lee Anne White; design: Derviss + Chavez Design + Build; (bottom) © Lee Anne White; Roger & Lisa Davenport residence; design: P.O.P.S. Landscaping

p. 108: (1) © Lee Anne White; (2) © Lee Anne White; design: Hillary Curtis, David Thorne Landscape Architects

p. 109: (3) © Lee Anne White; design: P.O.P.S. Landscaping; (4) © Lee Anne White; design: Desert Sage Builders

p. 110: (top) © Lee Anne White; (bottom) © Lee Anne White; design: Simply Outdoorz

p. 111: (left) © Mark Lohman; (right) © Lee Anne White; design: P.O.P.S. Landscaping

p. 112: (1) © Lee Anne White; design: Jennifer Romberg Designs & Jane Taylor/Cottage Garden Antiques; (2) © Lee Anne White

p. 113: (3, 4, and 5) © Lee Anne White

p. 114: (top) Lee Anne White; design: Simply Outdoorz; (bottom) © Lee Anne White; Phillip and Pat Bullard residence; design: WaterColors

p. 115: © Lee Anne White; Phillip and Pat Bullard residence; design: WaterColors

p. 116: © Lee Anne White; design: The Mad Hatter

p. 117: (top) © Lee Anne White; design: Derviss + Chavez Design + Build; (bottom) © Lee Anne White; design: Simply Outdoorz

p. 118: © Tim Street-Porter

p. 119: (top)© Lee Anne White: San Tran residence; design: Richard McPherson; (bottom) © Lee Anne White; design: Hillary Curtis, David Thorne Landscape Architects

p. 121: © Mark Lohman

p. 122: (1) © Saxon Holt; (2) © Lee Anne White; design: J.C. Enterprise Services, Inc.

p. 123: (3) © Lee Anne White; design: Simply Outdoorz; (4) © Tria Giovan

p. 124: (1) © Scott Zimmerman; (2) © Lee Anne White; design: Desert Sage Builders

p. 125: (3) © Lee Anne White; (4) © Lee Anne White; design: Derviss + Chavez Design + Build

p. 126: (1) © Lee Anne White; (2) © Lee Anne White

p. 127: (3) © Lee Anne White; design: Simply Outdoorz; (4) © Lee Anne White; courtesy Barbecues Galore

p. 128: (top & bottom) © Lee Anne White; Roger & Lisa Davenport residence; design: P.O.P.S. Landscaping

p. 129: © Lee Anne White; Dr. & Mrs. Timothy McComas residence; design: Desert Sage Builders

p. 130: (top) © Lee Anne White; design: Simmonds & Associates, Inc.; (bottom) © Lee Anne White; design: P.O.P.S. Landscaping

p. 131: © Lee Anne White; design: P.O.P.S. Landscaping

p. 132: (1) © Lee Anne White; Larry & Debbie Niffin residence; design: P.O.P.S. Landscaping; (2) © Lee Anne White; Hillary Curtis, David Thorne Landscape Architects

p. 133: (3) © Mark Lohman; (4) © Lee Anne White; design: Derviss + Chavez Design + Build

p. 134–135: © Lee Anne White

CHAPTER 5

p. 136: © Lee Anne White; design: Jon Carloftis

p. 138: © Tria Giovan

p. 139: (top) © Art Gray; (bottom) © Lee Anne White; design: P.O.P.S. Landscaping

p. 140–141: © Lee Anne White; design: Jeni Webber

p. 142: © Tim Street-Porter

p. 143: © Lee Anne White; design: Derviss + Chavez Design + Build

p. 144: (top) © Lee Anne White; Dr. & Mrs. Timothy McComas residence; design: Desert Sage Builders; (bottom) © Lee Anne White; design: Jeni Webber

p. 145: © Lee Anne White; design: James Bairey, Forno Bravo

p. 146: (top) © Allan Mandell; (bottom) © Lee Anne White; design: Hermann Weis

p. 147: (left) Brian Pontolilo, courtesy *Fine Homebuilding*, © The Taunton Press, Inc.; (right) © Lee Anne White; Eddie & Melissa Colvin residence; design: P.O.P.S. Landscaping

p. 148–149: © Lee Anne White; Meghan & Michael Zimmerman residence; architect: Eric Miketen; landscape design: Four Dimensions Landscape Co.

p. 150: (top) © Lee Anne White; design: P.O.P.S. Landscaping; (bottom) © Lee Anne White

p. 151: (top) © Lee Anne White; design: The Fockele Garden Company; (bottom) © Lee Anne White; design: Betty Romberg

p. 152: (1) © Lee Anne White; landscape design: WaterColors; (2) © Lee Anne White; Paul & Jacqui Peace residence; design: Twombly Nursery

p. 153: (3) © Tim Street-Porter

p. 154: © Lee Anne White; design: JC Enterprise Services

p. 155: (left) © Art Gray; (right) © Lee Anne White; Debbie & Larry Niffin residence; design: P.O.P.S. Landscaping

p. 156: (1 & 2) © Lee Anne White; design: Jennifer Romberg Interior Design

p. 157: (3 & 4) © Lee Anne White

CHAPTER 6

p. 158: © Mark Lohman

p. 160: © Lee Anne White; design: Louise Poer

p. 161: © Lee Anne White

p. 162: © Allan Mandell

p. 163: (top) © Saxon Holt; (bottom left) © Art Gray; (bottom right) © Lee Anne White; design: Michelle Derviss

p. 164: (top) © Lee Anne White; design: Enchantment Custom Builders; (bottom) © Lee Anne White; Dr. & Mrs. Timothy McComas residence; design: Desert Sage Builders

p. 165: (top) © CorrectDeck; (bottom) © Lee Anne White; design: P.O.P.S. Landscaping

P. 166: © Art Gray

p. 167: (top) © Lee Anne White; design: Hillary Curtis, David Thorne Landscape Architects; (bottom) © Anne Gummerson

p. 168: (top and bottom) © Allan Mandell

p. 169: © Lee Anne White; Wilson & Jenna Scanlan residence; design: Clemens & Associates

p. 170: © Scott Zimmerman

p. 171: (top) © Lee Anne White; design: Hillary Curtis & David Thorne, David Thorne Landscape Architects; (bottom) © Lee Anne White; Ed & Susan Goodwin residence; design: Twombly Nursery

p. 172: (top) © Lee Anne White; design: Jennifer Romberg Interior Design; (bottom) © Lee Anne White; design: Jennifer Romberg Interior Design

p. 173: (top) © Lee Anne White; design: Jennifer Romberg Interior Design; artist: Jane Taylor/ Cottage Garden Antiques; (bottom) © Lee Anne White; design: Jennifer Romberg Interior Design

p. 174: (top) © Lee Anne White; Eddie & Melissa Colvin residence; design: P.O.P.S. Landscaping; (bottom) © Lee Anne White

p. 175: © Lee Anne White

p. 176: © Lee Anne White; design: Hillary Curtis, David Thorne Landscape Architects

p. 177: © Lee Anne White

P. 178: (1 and 2) © Lee Anne White

p. 179: (3) © Tim Street-Porter; (4) © Lee Anne White; Eddie & Melissa Colvin residence; design: P.O.P.S. Landscaping

p. 180: © Tim Street-Porter

p. 181: (top left) © Scott Zimmerman; (top right) © Lee Anne White; design: P.O.P.S. Landscaping; (bottom) © Saxon Holt

p. 182: (top) © Lee Anne White; design: Enchantment Custom Builders; (bottom) © Lee Anne White; Roger & Lisa Davenport residence; design: P.O.P.S. Landscaping

p. 183: (left) © Mark Turner; (right) © Lee Anne White

p. 184: (1) © Lee Anne White; Paul D. Okerberg residence; design: John Willis Homes; (2) © Lee Anne White; design: Derviss + Chavez Design + Build

p. 185: (3) © Lee Anne White; design: P.O.P.S. Landscaping; (4) © Lee Anne White; (5) © Lee Anne White; design: Michelle Derviss

pp. 186–187: © Lee Anne White; design: Derviss + Chavez Design + Build

p. 188: © Lee Anne White; design: WaterColors

p. 189: (top) © www.carolynbates.com; (bottom left) © Scott Zimmerman; (bottom right) © Lee Anne White

p. 190: (top) courtesy Seaside Casual; (bottom) © Lee Anne White; design: Robert Norris

p. 191: © Mark Turner

p. 192: © Scott Zimmerman

p. 193: © Lee Anne White

P. 194: (1) © Lee Anne White

p. 195: (2) © Tim Street-Porter; (3) © Lee Anne White; Eddie & Melissa Colvin residence; design: P.O.P.S. Landscaping

p. 196: (top) © Lee Anne White; design: Robert Norris; (bottom) © Lee Anne White; design: Jennifer Romberg Interior Design & Jane Taylor/Cottage Garden Antiques

p. 197: (top) © Lee Anne White; (bottom) © Lee Anne White; design: Dan Cleveland & Jeffrey Rogerson

p. 198: (1) © Lee Anne White; sculpture: Katy McFadden; (2) © Lee Anne White; design: Fred & Sallye Hook

p. 199: (3) © Lee Anne White; Gail Giffen garden; design: Four Dimensions Landscape Co.; sculpture: Marcia Donahue; (4) © Lee Anne White; design: Joan Lewis

p. 200: © Lee Anne White

p. 201: © Lee Anne White; design: Desert Sage Builders

p. 202: (1) © Lee Anne White; design: Keeyla Meadows; (2) © Lee Anne White; design: David Feix

p. 203: (3) © Lee Anne White; (4) © Lee Anne White; design: Robert Norris

p. 204: (1) © Lee Anne White; design: The Fockele Garden Company; (2) © Lee Anne White; Ed and Susan Goodwin residence; design: Twombly Nursery

p. 205: (3) © Lee Anne White; design: The Fockele Garden Company; (4) © Lee Anne White; design: David Feix; (5) © Lee Anne White; design: Naomi Sachs

INDEX

KITCHEN IDEAS THAT WORK

Beth Veillette
Paperback
ISBN 13: 978-156158-837-4
ISBN10: 1-56158-837-7
EAN: 9781561588374
9 x 10 ½
240 pages
382 full color photographs
   throughout
27 drawings
Product # 070883
$19.95 U.S., $25.95 Can.
Available

BATHROOM IDEAS THAT WORK

Scott Gibson
Paperback
ISBN 13: 978-156158-836-7
ISBN10: 1-56158-836-9
EAN: 9781561588367
9 x 10 ½
224 pages
367 full color photographs
   throughout
17 drawings
Product # 070884
$19.95 U.S., $25.95 Can.
Available

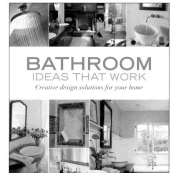

DECORATING IDEAS THAT WORK

Heather J. Paper
Paperback
ISBN 13: 978-156158-950-0
ISBN10: 1-56158-950-0
EAN: 9781561589500
9 x 10½
288 pages
475 full color photographs
throughout
30 drawings
Product # 070962
$21.95 U.S., $27.95 Can.
Available October 2007

OUTDOOR KITCHEN IDEAS THAT WORK

Lee Anne White
Paperback
ISBN 13: 978-156158-958-6
ISBN10: 1-56158-958-6
EAN: 9781561589586
9 x 10 ½
224 pages
350 full color photographs
   throughout
30 drawings
Product # 070968
$19.95 U.S., $25.95 Can.
Available January 2008

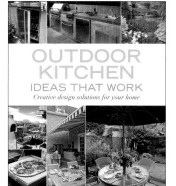

BASEMENT IDEAS THAT WORK

Peter Jeswald
Paperback
ISBN 13: 978-1-56158-937-1
ISBN10: 1-56158-937-3
EAN: 9781561589371
9 x 10 ½
184 pages
243 full color photographs
   throughout
20 drawings
Product #070941
$19.95 U.S., $25.95 Can.
Available January 2008

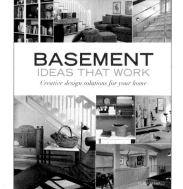